BARRIERS TO BREAKTHROUGH

BARRIERS TO BREAKTHROUGH

13 Strategies for Effective Leadership In The Multi-generational Workplace

Dr. Don Wilkins

Copyright © 2024 by Transformation 180, LLC.

ISBN Hardcover: 979-8-9922486-0-9
ISBN Softcover: 979-8-9922486-1-6
E-book: 979-8-9922486-2-3
Audio book: 979-8-9922486-3-0

All rights reserved. No part of this book may be reproduced or transmitted in any form or by any means, electronic or mechanical, including photocopying, recording, or by any information storage and retrieval system, without permission in writing from the copyright owner.

Dr. Don Wilkins
don@transformation180.org
P.O Box 12 Homestead, PA 15120

Transformation 180, LLC

ACKNOWLEDGMENTS

This book would not have been possible without the unwavering support, collaboration, and patience of some very special people in my life.

To **Danielle**—my thought partner, my sounding board, and my voice of reason. Your invaluable input and encouragement pushed me to dig deeper, refine my ideas, and stay focused on the goal. Thank you for helping me shape this work into something I'm truly proud of.

To **Stoney and Edwards**—thank you for being my "guinea pigs" as I tested out ideas, strategies, and concepts. Your willingness to engage, give feedback, and roll with the process gave me the confidence to turn these insights into something meaningful.

And to everyone who contributed to this journey—whether through your insights, challenges, or inspiration—thank you. Leadership is not a solitary pursuit, and this book is a reflection of the collective lessons I've learned from the incredible people around me.

With gratitude,
Don

ABOUT THE AUTHOR

Dr. Don Wilkins is an educator, leader, and advocate for transformational change in schools. With over 15 years of experience, he has served students, teachers, and communities across multiple cities, including Chicago, Atlanta, and Pittsburgh, bringing a steadfast commitment to empowering individuals, breaking barriers, and fostering growth—especially in schools facing significant challenges.

Dr. Wilkins's career in education has been marked by diversity and depth. He began as a paraprofessional, where he experienced the critical importance of support systems for both teachers and students. As a classroom teacher, he honed the art of effective instruction and recognized the transformative power of building strong relationships to inspire success. His work as a mentor teacher and residency/induction coach enabled him to guide educators at various career stages, instilling confidence and elevating instructional practices to drive student achievement.

As an Assistant Principal and Lead Principal, Dr. Wilkins developed expertise in school leadership and organizational change. He led Turnaround and CSI-designated schools, successfully removing these institutions from failing state lists and transforming them into vibrant centers of learning, hope, and achievement. His leadership has consistently demonstrated that no school is too far gone, no team too fractured, and no student beyond reach when guided by strong and compassionate leadership.

Dr. Wilkins has been formally trained in the School Turnaround Model, effective teacher and leader coaching models, and the Danielson Framework for teaching. These tools have enabled him to identify barriers, implement targeted strategies, and elevate both instructional quality and student outcomes.

Dr. Wilkins is currently the founder of Transformation 180, a consulting firm dedicated to helping schools achieve lasting improvement. Through Transformation 180, he travels the country partnering with schools and districts on their turnaround initiatives. His work involves coaching leaders, implementing research-based strategies, and fostering collective efficacy among staff to create sustainable success. His expertise has made him a trusted advisor to educational leaders who seek to transform their institutions and elevate student outcomes. Through Transformation 180, Dr. Wilkins has expanded his impact beyond the walls of a single school, helping countless educators and students across the nation benefit from his expertise and vision.

His work in education has earned him numerous accolades. Dr. Wilkins is a recipient of the Excellence in Education Award presented by the State of Black Learning, recognizing his transformative contributions to education. His leadership has been highlighted in the Pittsburgh City Paper and featured on the WPXI television network, bringing visibility to the critical importance of equity and leadership in schools.

Why This Book?

This book reflects Dr. Wilkins's journey—a culmination of lessons learned through successes, challenges, and a relentless pursuit of progress. He wrote this book to address the critical role leadership plays in breaking barriers to success and to provide practical tools and strategies for leaders to empower their teams, foster collaboration, and create thriving environments where both staff and students excel.

Dr. Wilkins believes that leadership is not merely about managing organizations; it is about transforming lives. His experiences leading schools and consulting with districts have shown him that the right leadership strategies, coupled with a deep understanding of individual and organizational needs, can achieve extraordinary outcomes.

This book serves as a guide and source of inspiration for leaders in education and beyond, equipping them to lead with purpose, clarity, and heart. Leadership, in Dr. Wilkins's view, is a calling that demands courage, vision, and an unwavering commitment to growth. Through this work, he invites readers to rise to the challenge of transforming their teams, schools, and communities for the better.

INTRODUCTION

Leadership in a Post-COVID World

The COVID-19 pandemic was a defining moment in modern history—a global disruption that tested leaders, organizations, and societies in unprecedented ways. The crisis demanded rapid adaptation, decisive action, and emotional resilience. Yet, as the dust settles, it has become clear that leadership in the post-COVID era is not simply about recovery; it is about reimagination, innovation, and building sustainable resilience for the future.

Leaders today are no longer operating in the world they knew before 2020. The pandemic accelerated shifts that were already underway, disrupted traditional ways of working, and revealed both strengths and vulnerabilities in leadership models across the globe. Remote work became not only a necessity but a long-term reality. Digital transformation went from a slow, deliberate process to an imperative completed in months. Mental health and emotional well-being moved from being peripheral concerns to core elements of organizational culture. And perhaps most importantly, employees and stakeholders alike began to demand purpose, empathy, and trust from their leaders like never before.

In this new landscape, the question is no longer whether leaders can manage disruption—it is how well they can thrive amid uncertainty and constant change. The traits and skills that made leaders successful in the past have evolved. Today's leaders must combine a strong vision for the future with a deep sense of humanity, balancing the pursuit of performance with a commitment to people.

Leadership Lessons from Crisis

The pandemic taught us profound lessons about leadership. It illuminated the power of adaptability—the ability to pivot quickly in response to challenges while maintaining organizational stability. It highlighted the importance of clear and empathetic communication at a time when confusion and fear were at their peak. Leaders who could inspire confidence and bring people together—even virtually—emerged stronger.

At the same time, COVID-19 exposed leadership shortcomings. Leaders who failed to listen, lacked empathy, or resisted change were quickly left behind. It became clear that effective leadership was not about holding onto power or rigid processes, but about empowering others, fostering collaboration, and building resilience across entire organizations.

The Post-COVID Leader: Key Shifts

As we move forward, the post-COVID leader must embrace a new mindset and set of skills:

1. **Empathy as a Core Leadership Competency:** COVID-19 was a deeply human crisis. It reminded leaders that their people are their most valuable assets. Compassion, emotional intelligence, and active listening are no longer "nice-to-haves"—they are essential for building trust, loyalty, and productivity.
2. **Adaptability and Agility:** Leaders must cultivate organizations that are agile and responsive to change. This means embracing experimentation, empowering teams to innovate, and being willing to pivot when needed.
3. **Digital Fluency:** Digital transformation is here to stay. Leaders must not only understand technology but also champion its integration into workflows, culture, and strategy to drive efficiency and innovation.
4. **Sustainability and Purpose:** Stakeholders increasingly expect organizations to address societal challenges such as

climate change, inequality, and diversity. Purpose-driven leadership—balancing profit with impact—is critical to building resilient and ethical organizations.

5. **Resilience Through Well-being:** The mental health crisis sparked by COVID-19 has brought well-being to the forefront. Leaders must prioritize psychological safety, encourage work-life balance, and foster supportive workplace cultures to ensure their teams can thrive in the long run.
6. **Distributed and Hybrid Leadership:** Remote and hybrid work are now permanent features of the workplace. Leaders must learn to inspire, engage, and lead distributed teams effectively while building a culture of belonging.

Leading Beyond the Crisis: A Deeper Perspective

While the immediate focus during COVID-19 was survival, the lessons we carry forward must inspire a rethinking of leadership norms. A post-COVID leader must look beyond temporary fixes and embrace systemic, future-ready solutions that address root challenges:

- **Investing in Human Capital:** Leaders must commit to upskilling and reskilling employees to prepare them for the digital economy. Workforce development programs,

mentorship initiatives, and lifelong learning pathways will be critical to ensuring organizations remain competitive and employees feel valued and empowered.
- **Reimagining Organizational Structures:** The traditional hierarchical model of leadership is giving way to flatter, more collaborative structures. Decision-making is increasingly decentralized, with leaders empowering teams to take ownership, innovate, and contribute to organizational success.
- **Leading with Transparency:** Trust is built on transparency. Post-pandemic leaders must communicate openly about challenges, progress, and decisions. Transparency fosters credibility, strengthens relationships with stakeholders, and ensures alignment around shared goals.
- **Nurturing Long-term Vision:** While short-term agility is essential, post-COVID leaders must also be architects of the long-term vision. Strategic foresight—anticipating trends, preparing for future disruptions, and building sustainable business models—is critical to success.

Building a Resilient Future

The post-COVID world is an era of opportunity for leaders willing to reimagine their roles and adapt to this transformed landscape. The challenges may be complex, but so too are the possibilities. Leaders who approach this moment with curiosity, courage, and conviction will not only lead their teams through uncertainty but will shape the future of their organizations and societies.

This book will explore the essential skills, strategies, and mindsets leaders need to navigate the post-COVID world. From fostering innovation to building trust and leading with purpose, it will provide actionable insights and real-world examples to help leaders thrive in an era of constant change.

The pandemic showed us that leadership is not about perfection. It is about progress. It is about showing up, listening, learning, and adapting. The future belongs to those who lead with vision, resilience, and humanity.

CONTENTS

Acknowledgments 5
About the Author 7
Introduction: Leadership in a Post-COVID World 11

1. The Pillars of Effective Leadership 19
2. The Coach vs. The Supervisor 28
3. Identifying and Addressing Barriers to Success 36
4. The Delegation Strategy as a Supervisor 41
5. The Deny/Approve Strategy as a Supervisor 49
6. The Inspection Strategy as a Supervisor 57
7. The Communication Strategy as a Supervisor 65
8. The Mentorship Strategy as a Coaching 74
9. The Suggestions Strategy as a Coach 82
10. The Modeling Strategy as a Coach 89
11. The Observation Strategy as a Coach 94
12. Acknowledgement as a Leadership Strategy for Capacity Barriers 102
13. Grace as a Leadership Strategy for Capacity Barriers 108
14. Scheduled Check-Ins as a Leadership Strategy for Capacity Barriers 116

15. Providing Professional Development as a Leadership Strategy for Knowledge Barriers.. 123
16. Providing Resources as a Leadership Strategy for Knowledge Barriers .. 131
17. Generational Workplace Values and Characteristics................................ 139
18. Empowering Leadership Through Generational Understanding and Strategies.. 147
19. Putting Strategies into Action 156
20. A Call to Action for Leaders of Today... 248

CHAPTER 1

The Pillars of Effective Leadership

Leadership is both an art and a discipline, requiring not only the ability to inspire and guide but also the capacity to execute with precision and purpose. In the post-COVID world, where uncertainty and rapid change dominate, truly effective leadership demands a holistic approach. Leaders must focus on more than their own vision; they must empower their organizations to thrive through collaboration, resilience, and a culture of excellence.

Leadership: A Responsibility, a Calling, and a Privilege

Leadership is not a position—it is a responsibility, a calling, and a privilege. True leaders understand that their role is not about titles or authority but about serving others, driving meaningful change, and creating a positive impact. This mindset transforms leadership from a task into a mission.

1. **A Responsibility to Others:** Leaders are entrusted with the growth, well-being, and success of their teams. It is their duty to guide, inspire, and remove obstacles that hinder progress.

2. **A Calling to Serve:** Leadership is a commitment to service—to putting the needs of the organization, its people, and its purpose above personal interests. It requires selflessness, humility, and dedication to empowering others.
3. **A Privilege to Lead:** Leading others is an honor that should never be taken for granted. Leaders have the unique opportunity to influence lives, shape futures, and leave behind a legacy of progress, trust, and inspiration.

Effective leaders recognize that their power comes not from their position but from the trust they earn and the relationships they nurture. They approach their work with gratitude and integrity, understanding the profound impact their decisions and actions have on others.

Leaders are Charged With:

Setting the Vision

At the heart of effective leadership lies a clear and compelling vision. A leader's vision serves as the guiding star, aligning teams and resources toward a shared purpose. Without a vision, organizations risk drifting aimlessly, reacting to challenges rather than proactively shaping the future.

1. **Define a Purpose-Driven Vision:** The most successful leaders craft visions that go beyond financial metrics and resonate on a human level. A purpose-driven vision connects the organization's goals to societal or individual impact, inspiring employees to find deeper meaning in their work.
2. **Communicate with Clarity and Passion:** A vision only becomes powerful when it is effectively communicated. Leaders must articulate their vision in ways that are both aspirational and actionable, ensuring that every team member understands how their role contributes to the broader goals.
3. **Adapt the Vision Over Time:** While staying true to core values, leaders must also recognize when external circumstances or internal priorities necessitate refining the vision. Agility in maintaining relevance without losing focus is critical to long-term success.
4. **Inspire Action:** A vision is only as impactful as the action it generates. Leaders must link their vision to measurable steps, motivating teams to transform aspirations into tangible results. The best leaders energize their people by showing how the vision ties directly to their day-to-day work.

Eliminating Barriers

Even the most inspired vision can falter if organizations are burdened by obstacles. Effective leaders actively work to identify and remove these barriers, enabling their teams to perform at their best.

1. **Streamline Decision-Making:** Complex hierarchies and bureaucratic processes can stifle creativity and delay progress. Leaders must simplify decision-making pathways, empowering teams to act with speed and confidence.
2. **Address Resource Constraints:** Whether it's time, budget, or tools, resource limitations can hinder progress. Leaders must allocate resources strategically, ensuring that teams have what they need to succeed.
3. **Foster Open Communication:** Silos and miscommunication often create unnecessary challenges. Effective leaders build a culture of transparency, encouraging feedback and collaboration across all levels of the organization.
4. **Challenge Limiting Mindsets:** Sometimes, the greatest barriers are mental rather than structural. Leaders must help teams overcome self-doubt, fear of failure, and resistance to change by fostering a growth mindset and celebrating calculated risk-taking.

5. **Remove Toxic Practices:** Barriers are not always visible. A lack of psychological safety, micromanagement, or fear of retribution can quietly undermine teams. Leaders must identify toxic practices and replace them with trust, autonomy, and open dialogue.
6. **Build Systems of Support:** Effective leaders put systems in place that allow teams to navigate challenges proactively. Whether through mentoring, access to tools, or providing space for creativity, these systems ensure teams have the foundations they need to excel.

Building Other Leaders

True leadership is not about singular success but about creating an environment where others can rise. Leaders who invest in building other leaders ensure that their organizations remain strong and adaptive over the long term.

1. **Mentor and Develop Talent:** Effective leaders identify potential in others and provide mentorship, training, and opportunities for growth. This not only strengthens the organization but also builds loyalty and engagement among employees.
2. **Delegate Meaningfully:** Delegation is more than assigning tasks; it's about entrusting others with responsibilities

that challenge and empower them. Leaders who delegate strategically create a culture of ownership and accountability.

3. **Encourage Diverse Leadership Styles:** Not all leaders look or think the same. Effective leaders recognize and nurture diverse approaches to leadership, ensuring a variety of perspectives contribute to organizational success.
4. **Celebrate Leadership at All Levels:** Leadership doesn't have to come with a title. Recognizing and encouraging leadership behaviors—such as initiative, problem-solving, and collaboration—at every level reinforces a culture of empowerment.
5. **Develop Succession Plans:** Effective leaders think about the future, not just the present. Identifying and preparing future leaders ensures continuity and resilience. By sharing knowledge and responsibilities, leaders create a sustainable legacy.
6. **Encourage Lifelong Learning:** The most successful leaders foster a culture of continuous development. By supporting leadership training, knowledge sharing, and skill development, they inspire teams to grow both personally and professionally.

Celebrating Wins, Big and Small

In the pursuit of long-term goals, it's easy to overlook the importance of celebrating achievements along the way. Recognizing and celebrating success—whether a major milestone or a small victory—builds morale, fosters momentum, and reinforces a culture of positivity.

1. **Acknowledge Individual Contributions:** While team achievements are important, individual efforts should also be recognized. Personalized appreciation—whether through a simple thank-you or a formal acknowledgment—goes a long way in boosting morale.
2. **Celebrate Milestones Along the Journey:** Large goals can take years to achieve, so breaking them into smaller milestones creates opportunities for celebration and keeps teams motivated.
3. **Make Recognition Meaningful:** Effective celebrations go beyond generic praise. Tailor recognition to the individual or team, ensuring it reflects the specific effort or achievement being honored.
4. **Share Success Stories:** Highlighting wins—whether through newsletters, meetings, or social media—reinforces the behaviors and values that led to success, creating a ripple effect of inspiration across the organization.

5. **Reinforce a Culture of Gratitude:** Leaders who regularly recognize and celebrate success create an environment of gratitude and optimism. This mindset helps teams maintain motivation and focus even in challenging times.
6. **Balance Celebration with Reflection:** While celebrating wins, effective leaders also reflect on the journey—what went well and what can be improved. This balance ensures that teams not only celebrate success but also grow from the experience.

The Leadership Legacy

Truly effective leadership leaves a lasting impact. By setting a vision, removing obstacles, building others, and celebrating progress, leaders not only achieve results but also create cultures of trust, resilience, and innovation. Their legacy is not the position they held but the progress they inspired—the leaders they built, the barriers they dismantled, and the people they uplifted along the way.

Effective leadership is not a singular event but a continuous journey. Leaders who focus on building systems of support, inspiring others, and celebrating progress create a thriving, forward-focused organization. As this book continues, we will explore practical strategies for embedding these principles into daily leadership practices. The journey to effective leadership is ongoing, but with the right focus and commitment, leaders can create a transformative and enduring impact.

CHAPTER 2

The Coach vs. The Supervisor

One of the greatest challenges leaders face is understanding and mastering the balance between two essential roles: the coach and the supervisor. Both roles are critical to effective leadership, but they require distinct mindsets, skill sets, and approaches. Knowing when to act as a coach and when to serve as a supervisor—and understanding the difficulty of being both at the same time—is key to building trust, achieving results, and fostering growth within a team.

Understanding the Difference

The Supervisor: A supervisor is task-focused and outcome-driven. They ensure accountability, oversee performance, and manage the completion of specific goals or objectives. Supervisors focus on the "what" and the "how," providing direction, structure, and corrective feedback when necessary.

- **Core Responsibilities:** Setting clear expectations, monitoring progress, solving problems, and holding individuals accountable for results.

- **Primary Focus:** Performance, timelines, and measurable outcomes.

The Coach: A coach, on the other hand, is growth-oriented and development-focused. Coaches empower individuals to unlock their potential, solve their own problems, and grow their skills through guidance, support, and reflection.

- **Core Responsibilities:** Asking powerful questions, providing constructive feedback, encouraging self-awareness, and facilitating learning.
- **Primary Focus:** Development, motivation, and long-term growth.

The key difference is that supervisors direct and manage performance, while coaches empower and inspire development. Both roles are necessary, but leaders must know which hat to wear in different situations.

When to Be a Supervisor

There are moments when a leader must adopt the role of a supervisor to ensure accountability and deliver results. Situations that demand structure, deadlines, and specific outcomes often call for a supervisor's mindset. Here are scenarios where the supervisory role is most effective:

1. **Meeting Critical Deadlines:** When tasks must be completed on time, a supervisor ensures that everyone stays on track and progress is measured.
2. **Addressing Performance Issues:** If performance falls short, leaders must step in as supervisors to identify gaps, provide corrective feedback, and set clear expectations.
3. **Clarifying Roles and Responsibilities:** Teams often need structure to function effectively. A supervisor defines roles, ensures accountability, and minimizes confusion.
4. **Managing High-Stakes Projects:** Projects that involve significant risk or tight timelines require a supervisory approach to ensure objectives are met.

In these scenarios, a leader's ability to provide clear direction, resolve issues quickly, and maintain focus on outcomes is vital for success.

When to Be a Coach

The coaching role, on the other hand, comes into play when the focus shifts to growth, learning, and long-term development. Coaching is essential for building the skills, confidence, and autonomy of team members. Situations that call for coaching include:

1. **Developing Future Leaders:** Coaching helps identify and nurture potential leaders by empowering them to take ownership of their growth and contributions.
2. **Encouraging Problem-Solving:** Instead of providing answers, a coach guides team members to think critically, reflect on challenges, and develop their own solutions.
3. **Fostering Personal and Professional Growth:** Coaching supports individuals in setting goals, building new skills, and gaining confidence in their abilities.
4. **Motivating Through Challenges:** In times of change or uncertainty, coaching inspires team members to embrace a growth mindset and navigate challenges with resilience.

By coaching, leaders invest in the long-term development of their teams, building stronger, more capable individuals who can thrive independently.

The Tension Between the Two Roles

One of the greatest difficulties leaders face is balancing the roles of coach and supervisor. At times, these roles can seem contradictory. For example, a supervisor's responsibility to correct behavior or enforce standards may feel at odds with a coach's role in fostering trust and encouraging autonomy. This tension can create challenges such as:

1. **Balancing Accountability with Empowerment:** While supervision requires holding people accountable for results, coaching requires trusting individuals to take ownership of their development. Striking the right balance is key.
2. **Switching Roles Seamlessly:** A leader may need to shift from supervisor to coach in the same conversation. For example, addressing a missed deadline (supervisor) may lead into a discussion about improving time management skills (coach).
3. **Managing Perceptions:** Team members may struggle to differentiate between the two roles. For example, feedback delivered as a coach may be interpreted as criticism from a supervisor. Leaders must clarify their intent and communicate transparently.
4. **Avoiding Micromanagement:** Leaders who default to the supervisory role risk stifling creativity and autonomy. True leadership requires knowing when to step back and allow team members to grow through coaching.

Mastering Both Roles

To be effective, leaders must develop the ability to fluidly transition between the roles of coach and supervisor based on the needs of the individual and the situation. Here are strategies for mastering both roles:

1. **Understand the Needs of the Moment:** Assess whether the situation calls for accountability (supervisor) or development (coach). Use performance metrics, team dynamics, and individual progress as a guide.
2. **Clarify Expectations:** Clearly communicate when you are providing direction as a supervisor versus when you are guiding as a coach. Team members will appreciate the clarity.
3. **Develop Emotional Intelligence:** Strong emotional intelligence allows leaders to read the needs of their team, provide the right level of support, and adjust their approach accordingly.
4. **Invest in Communication Skills:** Supervisors must provide clear, actionable feedback, while coaches must ask thoughtful questions that spark self-reflection and growth.
5. **Adopt a Growth Mindset:** Leaders who see every challenge as an opportunity to learn and grow can better

balance supervision and coaching. When correcting performance, frame it as an opportunity for development.
6. **Practice Consistency and Fairness:** Whether acting as a coach or supervisor, leaders must maintain fairness and consistency in their approach to build trust and credibility.

Integrating Coaching and Supervision into Leadership

The most effective leaders understand that coaching and supervision are not mutually exclusive. Instead, they complement each other. Leaders who integrate both roles effectively create a culture of accountability and empowerment, where individuals are held to high standards while being supported in their growth.

- **Supervision Ensures Results:** By setting clear expectations, monitoring progress, and addressing issues, supervision ensures that the team meets its goals.
- **Coaching Builds Capability:** By investing in development and empowering individuals, coaching strengthens the team's capacity to deliver results sustainably.

Leaders who master this integration create resilient, high-performing teams that thrive under any circumstances.

Final Thoughts

> Balancing the roles of coach and supervisor is one of the most complex yet rewarding aspects of leadership. While supervision ensures that goals are met today, coaching prepares teams for success tomorrow. Effective leaders recognize that both roles are essential and are skilled at navigating the tension between accountability and empowerment.
>
> Leadership is not about choosing between coaching and supervising; it is about knowing when and how to apply each role to bring out the best in individuals and teams. By mastering this balance, leaders can create an environment of trust, growth, and achievement—one where people feel supported to perform at their best and inspired to reach their fullest potential.

CHAPTER 3

Identifying and Addressing Barriers to Success

One of a leader's most critical responsibilities is helping their team overcome barriers that hinder success. However, identifying the root cause of these barriers requires careful analysis and discernment. A skilled leader understands that barriers often fall into one of four categories: **skill issues, will issues, knowledge issues, or capacity issues**. By identifying the correct issue, leaders can apply the appropriate strategy to resolve it effectively and empower their teams to move forward.

Understanding the Four Types of Barriers

1. **Skill Issues:** These barriers arise when an individual lacks the necessary skills to perform a task effectively. For example, a team member may struggle with a new software program, communication, or time management.
   - *Signs:* Frequent mistakes, incomplete work, or slow progress despite effort.
   - *Solution:* Provide targeted training, mentorship, or opportunities to practice and refine the skill. Leverage

strengths-based development to help individuals improve and apply skills where they can succeed.
2. **Will Issues:** Will issues occur when individuals lack motivation, engagement, or commitment to completing their work. This can stem from unclear goals, personal challenges, or dissatisfaction with their role.
    - *Signs:* Low energy, poor attitude, procrastination, or lack of initiative.
    - *Solution:* Leaders must identify the underlying cause of disengagement, reframe the work's purpose, and inspire individuals to reconnect with their mission. Sometimes, meaningful recognition or aligning work with personal goals can reignite motivation.
3. **Knowledge Issues:** Sometimes, team members lack the necessary information or understanding to complete a task. This may include missing processes, unclear expectations, or insufficient onboarding.
    - *Signs:* Confusion, repeated questions, incomplete or misdirected work.
    - *Solution:* Ensure that team members have access to the resources, information, and training they need to succeed. Clear communication, detailed documentation, and proactive check-ins help bridge knowledge gaps.

4. **Capacity Issues:** Capacity barriers arise when individuals are overwhelmed or do not have the time, tools, or bandwidth to complete their responsibilities effectively.
   - *Signs:* Burnout, high stress, missed deadlines, or an inability to focus.
   - *Solution:* Leaders must evaluate workloads, prioritize tasks, eliminate unnecessary work, and provide support. Redistributing responsibilities or bringing in additional resources can help restore balance and productivity.

Diagnosing the Root Cause

Before addressing a barrier, leaders must first diagnose the root cause accurately. Ask yourself the following questions:

- Does this team member lack the **skills** required to meet expectations?
- Is there a lack of **will** or motivation to perform the work?
- Is this a **knowledge** issue stemming from unclear instructions or missing information?
- Are there **capacity** concerns, such as time constraints or resource shortages?

By systematically assessing these areas, leaders can address the true barrier and avoid ineffective solutions.

Leading Through Barriers

Once a leader identifies the root cause, they must act decisively to provide the right support. Whether through coaching, supervision, or resourcing, the leader's role is to remove barriers, build capability, and inspire progress. Effective leaders don't just solve problems; they equip their team to overcome future challenges independently.

To lead through barriers effectively:

1. **Ask Questions:** Engage with team members to understand their challenges and perspective. Open communication builds trust and helps uncover hidden issues.
2. **Tailor Your Approach:** Match the solution to the root cause. For skill issues, offer training; for capacity issues, redistribute workloads. One-size-fits-all solutions rarely work.
3. **Build Resilience:** Use barriers as opportunities to develop problem-solving skills within the team. Encourage ownership and accountability in addressing challenges.

4. **Celebrate Breakthroughs:** Acknowledge when individuals or teams overcome barriers. Recognizing progress builds confidence and reinforces positive behavior.

Barriers as Leadership Opportunities

Every barrier presents an opportunity for growth—not just for individuals but for the leader as well. Addressing barriers requires leaders to sharpen their diagnostic skills, demonstrate empathy, and adapt their strategies to meet the needs of their teams. By confronting barriers head-on, leaders build stronger, more resilient teams that can achieve exceptional results.

The most effective leaders don't shy away from challenges. Instead, they view barriers as moments to teach, inspire, and elevate the people around them. By understanding the nature of the barrier—whether it's a skill issue, will issue, knowledge issue, or capacity issue—leaders can empower their teams to overcome obstacles and thrive in any environment.

In the end, leadership is about enabling success. It's about removing obstacles, providing support, and helping people grow into the best versions of themselves. By mastering this ability, leaders build teams that are not only productive but also inspired, resilient, and capable of achieving greatness.

CHAPTER 4

The Delegation Strategy as a Supervisor

Effective leadership requires the ability to address barriers head-on, and for leaders operating as supervisors, delegation is one of the most powerful strategies available. Delegation is not merely a way to offload tasks—it is an intentional act of empowering team members, developing their skills, and ensuring the leader's focus remains on high-value priorities. For leaders addressing barriers such as capacity, knowledge gaps, or skill development needs, delegation serves as a critical tool for maintaining efficiency and fostering growth.

The Importance of Delegation

Delegation enables leaders to address challenges on multiple fronts:

1. **Maximizing Capacity:** Leaders cannot do everything themselves. By distributing tasks appropriately, delegation ensures that workloads are balanced and no single individual—including the leader—becomes overwhelmed.

2. **Skill Development:** Delegating new responsibilities provides team members with opportunities to grow, learn, and build confidence in their abilities.
3. **Increasing Efficiency:** Leaders can focus on strategic, high-level tasks by entrusting day-to-day responsibilities to capable team members.
4. **Building Trust:** When leaders delegate effectively, they communicate trust in their team's abilities, fostering stronger relationships and greater engagement.
5. **Driving Innovation:** Delegating creative tasks and problem-solving initiatives allows team members to contribute fresh ideas and perspectives, fueling innovation and growth.

What to Delegate

Leaders acting as supervisors can delegate a variety of tasks, initiatives, and responsibilities, such as:

1. **Tasks:** Routine administrative duties, data entry, or recurring reports that do not require the leader's direct involvement.
2. **Initiatives:** Special projects or programs that align with team members' skills and development goals.

3. **Projects:** Specific, time-bound objectives such as launching a new product, organizing an event, or implementing a new process.
4. **Events:** Coordinating team-building activities, client presentations, or community outreach events.
5. **Problem-Solving Activities:** Assigning ownership of challenges and encouraging individuals to propose solutions to operational or team-related issues.
6. **Strategic Research:** Asking team members to investigate trends, gather market insights, or explore potential improvements for workflows or systems.

By identifying opportunities to delegate, leaders can ensure their focus remains on areas where their expertise and decision-making are most needed.

The Delegation Process

Effective delegation is a skill that requires thoughtfulness and intentionality. Here are the key steps:

1. **Identify the Task:** Determine what can be delegated by evaluating the nature of the task, its complexity, and the expertise required to complete it.

2. **Select the Right Person:** Match the task to a team member whose skills, interests, and workload align with the responsibility. Delegation should be an opportunity for growth—not a burden.
3. **Define Expectations:** Clearly outline the task's objectives, deliverables, deadlines, and any critical resources. Provide the context needed for the individual to understand the task's importance.
4. **Empower and Equip:** Ensure the individual has the tools, resources, and authority to complete the task. Remove any barriers that may impede their success.
5. **Monitor Progress:** Check in periodically to provide support and ensure the task is on track. Avoid micromanaging, but remain available to answer questions or provide guidance as needed.
6. **Provide Feedback:** Once the task is completed, offer constructive feedback. Recognize achievements and highlight areas for improvement to facilitate learning.
7. **Celebrate Success:** Acknowledge the individual's efforts and results. Celebrate successes publicly to build confidence and reinforce the value of their contributions.

Overcoming Delegation Barriers

Leaders often hesitate to delegate for several reasons: fear of losing control, lack of trust in their team, or a belief that they can complete the task faster themselves. To overcome these barriers, leaders should:

1. **Shift Their Mindset:** View delegation as an investment in their team rather than a loss of control. Empowering others leads to greater overall productivity.
2. **Start Small:** Begin by delegating low-risk tasks and gradually expand responsibilities as team members build confidence and demonstrate reliability.
3. **Develop Trust:** Trust is earned over time. By delegating tasks and providing the necessary support, leaders can build trust with their team.
4. **Focus on Development:** Recognize that delegation is not just about task completion—it is an opportunity to develop team members and prepare them for greater responsibilities.
5. **Let Go of Perfection:** Understand that team members may approach tasks differently. As long as the results meet expectations, empower them to use their own methods.

6. **Empower Autonomy:** Give team members ownership of the work and encourage them to take initiative in achieving the desired outcomes.

The Supervisory Role in Delegation

Delegation requires leaders to wear their supervisory hat effectively. While the process involves entrusting responsibilities to others, the leader remains accountable for the outcome. This means:

1. **Setting Clear Goals:** Supervisors must ensure that the delegated tasks align with organizational objectives.
2. **Providing Structure:** Offer guidance and establish a framework for how the task should be completed without dictating every step.
3. **Ensuring Accountability:** Hold team members accountable for their commitments while providing the support needed to achieve success.
4. **Celebrating Wins:** Acknowledge and celebrate accomplishments, both big and small, to reinforce positive behavior and motivate the team.
5. **Balancing Oversight with Autonomy:** Leaders must strike a balance between offering oversight and allowing team members the space to operate independently.

Benefits of Delegation for the Team

When done effectively, delegation doesn't just benefit the leader—it transforms the team as well. Delegation:

1. **Builds Confidence:** Team members feel empowered when they are entrusted with new responsibilities and see their work contributing to larger goals.
2. **Strengthens Engagement:** Delegated work fosters ownership and commitment, as individuals take pride in achieving results.
3. **Promotes Skill Growth:** By tackling new challenges, team members develop competencies and expand their capabilities.
4. **Encourages Collaboration:** Delegation often requires teamwork, helping individuals build stronger working relationships and improve communication.
5. **Prepares Future Leaders:** Delegation provides a platform for individuals to prove themselves, preparing them for greater leadership roles.

Final Thoughts

Delegation is more than a supervisory tool; it is a leadership strategy that drives efficiency, empowers teams, and creates a culture of shared responsibility. By mastering the art of delegation, leaders can address barriers such as capacity and skill gaps while building a stronger, more capable team.

Effective leaders understand that they cannot do everything themselves. Through delegation, they not only achieve results but also inspire growth, build trust, and create an environment where every team member can contribute to the organization's success. In the end, successful delegation is not about relinquishing control—it is about multiplying a leader's impact and empowering the team to achieve greatness together.

CHAPTER 5

The Deny/Approve Strategy as a Supervisor

Leaders often find themselves in the position of evaluating ideas, requests, and suggestions from their teams. While the act of denying or approving a proposal may seem straightforward, it is a nuanced leadership strategy that requires consideration, communication, and empathy. This strategy is particularly effective when staff members encounter barriers, as it enables leaders to maintain organizational alignment while fostering clarity and trust.

Understanding the Deny/Approve Strategy

The deny/approve strategy involves making deliberate decisions about requests, ideas, or suggestions that staff members bring forward. It requires leaders to assess the merit of each proposal, determine its alignment with organizational goals, and provide clear, constructive feedback. By doing so, leaders address barriers such as unclear expectations, limited capacity, or misaligned priorities. At its core, this strategy must be rooted in aligning every decision with the vision and mission of the organization.

This strategy is also particularly relevant for addressing issues with unruly or disconnected staff members who are not aligning with the organization's vision or mission. In such cases, the deny/approve approach provides a structured way to guide behavior, enforce standards, and recalibrate focus on the organization's goals.

The deny/approve strategy encompasses three key components:

1. **Evaluating Proposals Thoughtfully:** Leaders must assess the potential impact, feasibility, and alignment of each request or idea with organizational goals.
2. **Communicating Decisions Clearly:** Whether a proposal is denied or approved, the leader's response must be clear, respectful, and constructive.
3. **Providing Guidance:** Leaders should use the opportunity to reinforce priorities, clarify expectations, and offer support for future proposals.

When to Deny

Denying a request or idea can be challenging, but it is often necessary to maintain focus and ensure resources are allocated effectively. Common reasons for denying include:

1. **Misalignment with Goals:** If the proposal does not support the organization's mission, vision, or strategic objectives.
2. **Capacity Constraints:** If the team lacks the time, resources, or skills needed to execute the proposal effectively.
3. **Inadequate Planning:** If the idea lacks a clear plan, measurable outcomes, or a realistic timeline.
4. **Conflicting Priorities:** If the proposal would divert attention from more critical initiatives or create unnecessary complexity.
5. **Behavioral Concerns:** When a proposal stems from unruly or disconnected staff members whose priorities do not align with the organization's core values or mission.

When denying a proposal, it is crucial for leaders to:

- **Explain the Reasoning:** Clearly articulate why the request is being denied, focusing on facts and organizational priorities.
- **Acknowledge the Effort:** Recognize the individual's initiative and the value of their contribution.
- **Offer Constructive Feedback:** Provide guidance on how the idea could be improved or aligned for future consideration.

Example:

> *"I appreciate the effort you put into this proposal. However, given our current focus on [specific priority], we're unable to move forward with this idea at this time. I encourage you to refine the concept by addressing [specific improvement], and we can revisit it in the future."*

When to Approve

Approving a proposal demonstrates trust and commitment to team members. Leaders should approve requests or ideas when they:

1. **Align with Organizational Goals:** The proposal supports the organization's mission, values, and strategic direction.
2. **Are Feasible:** The team has the capacity, resources, and skills needed to execute the idea successfully.
3. **Show Potential for Growth:** The proposal offers opportunities for innovation, improvement, or development within the organization.
4. **Are Well-Thought-Out:** The idea includes a clear plan, defined outcomes, and realistic timelines.

When approving a proposal, leaders should:

- **Celebrate the Idea:** Acknowledge the individual's contribution and the value of their proposal.
- **Define Next Steps:** Clearly outline the plan for implementation, including roles, timelines, and expectations.
- **Provide Support:** Offer resources, guidance, or mentorship to ensure successful execution.

Example:

> *"This is an excellent idea, and it aligns perfectly with our goals for [specific objective]. Let's move forward with this plan. I'll work with you to outline the next steps and ensure you have the support you need to succeed."*

Balancing the Deny/Approve Strategy

Leaders must strike a balance between denying and approving proposals to ensure their decisions:

1. **Promote Clarity:** Provide team members with a clear understanding of priorities, expectations, and decision-making criteria.

2. **Build Trust:** Demonstrate fairness, transparency, and respect in all decisions.
3. **Encourage Innovation:** Foster a culture where team members feel safe sharing ideas, even if some are not approved.
4. **Strengthen Alignment:** Ensure all proposals support the organization's long-term goals and values.

Addressing Barriers Through the Deny/Approve Strategy

The deny/approve strategy can help leaders address various barriers:

1. **Skill Barriers:** Approve opportunities for skill development, such as training or mentorship programs, while denying initiatives that require unprepared staff without proper support.
2. **Will Barriers:** Deny requests that stem from lack of commitment or effort, while approving initiatives that demonstrate enthusiasm and alignment with organizational goals.
3. **Knowledge Barriers:** Approve proposals that enhance knowledge-sharing or learning, while denying initiatives based on misinformation or incomplete understanding.

4. **Capacity Barriers:** Approve requests that balance workloads effectively, while denying proposals that overextend the team or compromise quality.

Rooting Decisions in Vision and Mission

At the heart of the deny/approve strategy lies a commitment to the organization's vision and mission. Every decision a leader makes—whether to deny or approve—should reinforce the organization's core purpose and strategic objectives. By consistently aligning proposals with these guiding principles, leaders:

- **Maintain Focus:** Keep the team centered on what truly matters to the organization's success.
- **Enhance Cohesion:** Ensure that all efforts contribute to a shared purpose, fostering unity and collaboration.
- **Build Credibility:** Demonstrate consistency and integrity in decision-making, reinforcing trust and respect among team members.

Final Thoughts

The deny/approve strategy is a powerful tool for leaders navigating the complexities of staff proposals and organizational priorities. By evaluating requests thoughtfully, communicating decisions clearly, and providing constructive guidance, leaders can build trust, foster innovation, and ensure alignment with organizational goals. Effective use of this strategy not only addresses barriers but also creates an environment where team members feel valued, supported, and inspired to contribute to the organization's success. Above all, leaders must remember that every decision is an opportunity to strengthen the organization's vision and mission, guiding the team toward a future of shared success.

CHAPTER 6

The Inspection Strategy as a Supervisor

In leadership, particularly within the supervisory role, one of the most effective strategies for addressing barriers is inspection. While inspection may sometimes carry negative connotations, when done with purpose, fairness, and focus, it becomes a critical tool for ensuring that expectations, requirements, and deliverables are being met. Inspection is not about micromanagement; it is about accountability, clarity, and support. Importantly, inspection is not a "gotcha moment" to catch staff in failure. Instead, it is a strategy designed to support individuals when they are experiencing barriers to success.

When staff members encounter barriers—whether they relate to skills, will, knowledge, or capacity—leaders need to determine whether the source of the problem lies in their execution of expectations. The inspection strategy allows leaders to target specific areas of concern, uncover underlying issues, and implement corrective action when necessary.

The Role of Inspection in Leadership

Inspection, as a supervisory strategy, is not random or generalized. It is:

1. **Targeted:** Focused on specific tasks, expectations, or deliverables where concerns have arisen.
2. **Objective:** Based on communicated standards, measurable outcomes, and clear requirements.
3. **Supportive:** Designed to help staff succeed by identifying barriers and offering corrective solutions.

Inspection is particularly vital when dealing with staff who are struggling to meet expectations, disconnected from the mission, or failing to deliver results. By inspecting specific areas of their work, leaders create opportunities to reinforce accountability, clarify misunderstandings, and provide guidance that helps the individual or team realign with organizational goals.

Inspecting Communicated Expectations

Leaders must first ensure that expectations have been clearly communicated before conducting inspections. Often, barriers arise because staff members do not fully understand what is expected of them or lack the tools to meet those expectations.

Effective inspection begins with revisiting the original communication to confirm that expectations are:

1. **Clear:** Stated in precise terms so there is no ambiguity.
2. **Specific:** Focused on measurable actions or deliverables.
3. **Time-Bound:** Linked to realistic deadlines.

If a barrier is discovered during inspection, leaders must consider whether the root cause is poor communication. When this occurs, leaders must take responsibility for restating expectations, ensuring alignment, and documenting what is required moving forward.

Example:

> *"I understand that the recent project did not meet the quality standards we agreed upon. Let's review the expectations together to ensure they are clear and achievable moving forward."*

Inspecting Requirements

Beyond expectations, leaders must also inspect whether staff members have the necessary requirements to succeed. Requirements refer to the tools, resources, or training that staff need to meet expectations. Barriers often occur when individuals are not properly equipped to execute tasks effectively.

When using the inspection strategy, leaders should:

1. **Evaluate Tools and Resources:** Do staff have access to the materials, technology, and systems they need to perform their work?
2. **Assess Training and Skills:** Are gaps in knowledge or skills creating performance barriers?
3. **Review Processes:** Are outdated or unclear processes hindering progress?

Leaders can use inspection to pinpoint areas where requirements are lacking and address those deficiencies. This may involve providing additional training, allocating resources, or streamlining systems.

Example:

> *"During our review of your progress, I noticed that the software system is creating delays in your workflow. Let's work on getting you the training or tools you need to use it more effectively."*

Inspecting Deliverables

The final component of inspection focuses on deliverables—the tangible results that staff members produce. Deliverables reflect whether expectations and requirements have been met. When inspecting deliverables, leaders must:

1. **Review Quality:** Does the work meet the expected standards of accuracy, professionalism, and effectiveness?
2. **Measure Timeliness:** Was the work delivered within the agreed timeframe?
3. **Ensure Alignment:** Does the work align with the organization's goals, mission, and priorities?

If deliverables fall short, inspection allows leaders to address the issue directly and determine whether the barrier stems from a skill issue, will issue, knowledge issue, or capacity issue. Leaders should use the opportunity to provide constructive feedback and corrective guidance.

Example:

> *"This report is a good starting point, but it doesn't fully address the key data we discussed in our planning meeting. Let's review the areas where improvement is needed so we can deliver the quality our stakeholders expect."*

Why Inspection is Critical for Barriers

The inspection strategy provides leaders with a structured way to address barriers while remaining fair, supportive, and results-oriented. It allows leaders to:

1. **Identify the Root Cause:** Inspection helps leaders determine whether a barrier is due to unclear expectations, missing requirements, or underperformance.
2. **Ensure Accountability:** Staff members remain accountable for their commitments and deliverables when they know their work will be reviewed objectively.
3. **Provide Timely Feedback:** By inspecting work at key milestones, leaders can offer feedback before barriers escalate into larger issues.
4. **Realign Staff with Goals:** Inspection provides an opportunity to reinforce the organization's mission and ensure that everyone remains focused on achieving shared objectives.

Inspection and the Supervisory Role

The inspection strategy is firmly rooted in the supervisory role of leadership. Leaders must maintain oversight of performance while balancing accountability with support. This is especially important when dealing with staff who are struggling or disconnected from the organization's vision.

Leaders can use targeted inspection as a means of:

- Addressing **Skill Barriers** by identifying gaps and recommending training or mentorship.
- Confronting **Will Barriers** by holding individuals accountable for meeting communicated expectations.
- Resolving **Knowledge Barriers** through clarification and support.
- Tackling **Capacity Barriers** by assessing workloads and reallocating tasks if necessary.

Balancing Inspection and Empowerment

While inspection is an essential supervisory strategy, leaders must strike a balance to avoid micromanagement. Inspection should focus on key deliverables, not every detail of an individual's work. To empower staff while implementing inspection, leaders should:

1. **Communicate Purpose:** Explain that inspection is about support, accountability, and success—not punishment.
2. **Collaborate on Solutions:** Use inspection findings to create action plans that empower staff to overcome barriers.

3. **Recognize Improvement:** Acknowledge progress when staff address issues identified during inspection.

Final Thoughts

> The inspection strategy is a powerful supervisory tool for addressing barriers and ensuring organizational alignment. By inspecting communicated expectations, requirements, and deliverables, leaders can identify root causes of performance issues and provide the support needed to overcome them. Inspection, when done thoughtfully and purposefully, fosters accountability, trust, and growth, ensuring that staff remain focused, equipped, and aligned with the organization's mission and vision.
>
> Leaders must remember that inspection is not about catching people in failure. It is about supporting their success. Through targeted and focused inspection, leaders can guide their teams to higher levels of performance, clarity, and success, while addressing barriers head-on in a supportive and constructive manner.

CHAPTER 7

The Communication Strategy as a Supervisor

When staff members experience barriers, a leader's ability to communicate effectively becomes one of the most crucial tools in the supervisory role. Clear, purposeful communication ensures alignment, accountability, and support, allowing the leader to address barriers proactively and guide the staff member toward success. Communication is not merely an exchange of information—it is a leadership strategy that bridges vision, expectations, and action.

This strategy involves four key components: communicating the vision, next steps, directives, and non-negotiables. While verbal communication is essential for immediate clarity and context, it should always be followed up with written communication, such as emails or formal documentation, to ensure mutual understanding and accountability.

The Supervisory Role of Communication

Effective communication is foundational to the supervisory role. Leaders must ensure that:

1. **The Vision is Clear:** Every staff member must understand how their role connects to the organization's overarching mission and objectives.
2. **Next Steps are Defined:** Concrete action plans and timelines eliminate ambiguity and provide a roadmap for overcoming barriers.
3. **Directives are Explicit:** Leaders must clearly articulate what is expected, why it is important, and how it should be executed.
4. **Non-Negotiables are Reinforced:** Staff must be made aware of behaviors, standards, or outcomes that are not open for compromise, particularly when they misalign with organizational values or goals.

Communicating the Vision

Staff members facing barriers often lose sight of the organization's broader purpose. Reconnecting them with the vision helps reignite their motivation and sense of responsibility. Leaders should:

- Share the organization's goals and priorities in a way that is relatable and relevant to the individual's role.
- Emphasize how their contributions impact the team, stakeholders, and the mission.
- Encourage a sense of ownership by linking tasks to meaningful outcomes.

Example:

> *"Your work on this project is crucial because it directly supports our goal of improving customer satisfaction. Let's discuss how we can address the current challenges so we can achieve that together."*

Outlining Next Steps

Barriers often create uncertainty about how to proceed. Leaders must eliminate this uncertainty by outlining clear, actionable next steps. These steps should be:

- **Specific:** Define exactly what needs to be done.
- **Time-Bound:** Include deadlines to create urgency and structure.
- **Achievable:** Ensure the steps are realistic given the staff member's current capacity and resources.

Example:

> *"To address the delay in this project, let's prioritize completing the draft report by next Wednesday. I'll review it with you the following day to finalize it for submission."*

Delivering Directives

When barriers stem from confusion or lack of direction, leaders must provide explicit directives. Directives are instructions that clarify expectations, ensuring that staff understand exactly what is required of them.

Key strategies for delivering directives:

1. **Be Concise:** Avoid overwhelming the individual with unnecessary information.
2. **Clarify Expectations:** Use plain language to describe desired outcomes.
3. **Invite Questions:** Encourage the staff member to seek clarification if needed.

Example:

> *"The presentation must include the sales data from the last quarter, a summary of trends, and three actionable recommendations. Please use the standard template, and let me know if you need help accessing the data."*

Reinforcing Non-Negotiables

Non-negotiables are the standards, policies, or values that must be upheld within the organization. When staff behavior or performance deviates from these, leaders must communicate firmly and without ambiguity.

Steps for reinforcing non-negotiables:

1. **State the Standard:** Remind the staff member of the policy, behavior, or outcome that is required.
2. **Address the Deviation:** Clearly explain how their current actions or results are falling short.
3. **Set Expectations:** Define what must change and the consequences of non-compliance.

Example:

> *"Punctuality for team meetings is a non-negotiable because it impacts everyone's ability to collaborate effectively. Arriving late disrupts the flow of discussion and delays progress. Moving forward, I expect you to be on time for every meeting. Continued tardiness may lead to further action."*

Verbal and Written Communication

While verbal communication is often the first step in addressing barriers, written communication solidifies understanding and accountability. Every significant conversation about expectations, performance, or corrective action should be followed up with written confirmation.

Why Written Communication Matters:

- **Clarity:** Ensures both parties have a record of what was discussed and agreed upon.
- **Accountability:** Provides documentation that can be referenced if issues persist.
- **Professionalism:** Demonstrates the leader's commitment to addressing barriers in a structured and respectful manner.

Example Email Follow-Up:

*Subject: Follow-Up on Our Conversation

Hi [Staff Member],

Thank you for taking the time to meet today to discuss [specific barrier or issue]. As we discussed, here are the key points:

1. [Expectation or directive]
2. [Next steps and deadlines]
3. [Any non-negotiables or consequences]

Please let me know if you have any questions or need further clarification. I'm here to support you as you work toward these goals.

Best regards,
[Leader's Name]*

Using Communication to Address Barriers

Effective communication directly addresses the four types of barriers:

1. **Skill Barriers:** Provide clear directives and offer training or resources as needed.
2. **Will Barriers:** Reconnect staff to the vision and reinforce non-negotiables to reignite commitment.
3. **Knowledge Barriers:** Outline next steps and clarify expectations to eliminate confusion.
4. **Capacity Barriers:** Collaborate on realistic action plans and adjust priorities where necessary.

Final Thoughts

> The communication strategy is a cornerstone of supervisory leadership. By consistently communicating the vision, next steps, directives, and non-negotiables, leaders can address barriers effectively while maintaining trust and accountability. Combining verbal and written communication ensures clarity, reinforces expectations, and provides staff with the structure they need to succeed.
>
> Leaders who master the art of communication create an environment where staff feel supported, aligned, and empowered to overcome challenges. This strategy not only addresses immediate barriers but also fosters long-term growth and organizational success.

CHAPTER 8

The Mentorship Strategy as a Coaching

One of the most impactful coaching strategies a leader can employ is mentorship. Unlike traditional supervision, which often focuses on tasks and outcomes, mentorship is deeply rooted in fostering personal and professional growth. It requires ongoing feedback, open communication, and a genuine investment in the success of the individual. Mentorship is not simply about giving advice; it is about sharing experiences and expertise in a way that motivates and empowers staff members to overcome barriers and achieve their potential.

The Essence of Mentorship

At its core, mentorship is a relationship built on trust, respect, and a shared commitment to growth. Effective mentorship requires the leader to step into the role of a guide—someone who:

- **Provides Support:** Mentors offer encouragement and emotional support, especially when staff members face challenges.

Final Thoughts

> The communication strategy is a cornerstone of supervisory leadership. By consistently communicating the vision, next steps, directives, and non-negotiables, leaders can address barriers effectively while maintaining trust and accountability. Combining verbal and written communication ensures clarity, reinforces expectations, and provides staff with the structure they need to succeed.
>
> Leaders who master the art of communication create an environment where staff feel supported, aligned, and empowered to overcome challenges. This strategy not only addresses immediate barriers but also fosters long-term growth and organizational success.

CHAPTER 8

The Mentorship Strategy as a Coaching

One of the most impactful coaching strategies a leader can employ is mentorship. Unlike traditional supervision, which often focuses on tasks and outcomes, mentorship is deeply rooted in fostering personal and professional growth. It requires ongoing feedback, open communication, and a genuine investment in the success of the individual. Mentorship is not simply about giving advice; it is about sharing experiences and expertise in a way that motivates and empowers staff members to overcome barriers and achieve their potential.

The Essence of Mentorship

At its core, mentorship is a relationship built on trust, respect, and a shared commitment to growth. Effective mentorship requires the leader to step into the role of a guide—someone who:

- **Provides Support:** Mentors offer encouragement and emotional support, especially when staff members face challenges.

- **Shares Expertise:** They draw on their own experiences and knowledge to help the mentee navigate similar situations.
- **Motivates and Inspires:** Mentors help mentees see their potential and find the drive to overcome barriers.

For staff members experiencing barriers, mentorship serves as a lifeline, offering them both practical tools and emotional reassurance to navigate difficulties.

Key Components of Effective Mentorship

1. **Ongoing Feedback and Communication** Feedback is central to mentorship. Regular, constructive communication helps mentees understand their progress, recognize areas for improvement, and build confidence. Mentorship conversations should:
   - Be consistent, with scheduled check-ins to discuss goals and challenges.
   - Include both positive reinforcement and actionable suggestions for growth.
   - Focus on specific examples and clear next steps to maintain clarity and momentum.
2. Example: *"I've noticed how much effort you've put into improving your presentation skills. Your last presentation was*

engaging, but let's work on tightening the timing for your next one. I'll share a technique I use to stay within the time limit."

3. **Sharing Experiences and Expertise** Mentors can be most effective when they share their own stories of overcoming challenges. This creates relatability and provides mentees with a roadmap for tackling their own barriers. Sharing experiences can include:
   - **Discussing Past Successes and Failures:** Sharing personal stories of both triumphs and setbacks demonstrates vulnerability and creates a learning opportunity. For example, a mentor might share a time they failed to meet a critical deadline, explain the lessons they learned, and describe how they adjusted their approach to succeed in the future. These stories show that mistakes are part of growth.
   - **Offering Practical Insights:** Mentors can provide specific strategies, tools, or frameworks that they have found effective. For instance, if a mentee struggles with time management, the mentor can introduce techniques like prioritization matrices, digital tools, or scheduling methods.
   - **Explaining Industry Trends and Dynamics:** By sharing their understanding of broader organizational or industry trends, mentors can help mentees

connect their individual roles to the bigger picture. For example, discussing how a specific skill set aligns with future industry demands can motivate a mentee to develop that skill.

- **Modeling Problem-Solving Techniques:** A mentor's ability to break down complex challenges and explain their thought process helps mentees develop critical thinking. Demonstrating how to approach a difficult decision or navigate workplace conflict equips mentees with practical approaches they can apply independently.

4. Example: *"Early in my career, I struggled with prioritizing tasks when everything felt urgent. One method that helped me was creating a matrix to categorize tasks by urgency and importance. Let me show you how it works."*

    - **Connecting Lessons to the Mentee's Journey:** By relating personal experiences directly to the mentee's current challenges, mentors make the lessons more relevant and impactful. For example, a mentor might say, "When I was in your position, I faced a similar challenge with project deadlines. Here's what I learned about breaking down the workload into smaller, manageable pieces."

5. **Motivating Through Encouragement** A mentor's belief in their mentee's potential can be a powerful motivator. Staff members experiencing barriers often need someone who sees their value and can remind them of their capabilities. Mentors motivate by:
    - Celebrating small wins to build momentum and confidence.
    - Helping mentees set and achieve realistic, meaningful goals.
    - Encouraging resilience by reframing challenges as opportunities for growth.
6. Example: *"I know this project feels overwhelming right now, but you've already made great progress in outlining the main steps. Let's focus on tackling one section at a time. You've got this."*

Benefits of Mentorship

When leaders adopt mentorship as a coaching strategy, the benefits extend beyond the individual mentee. Effective mentorship:

- **Builds Competence:** Staff members gain new skills, insights, and strategies to overcome barriers.

- **Strengthens Relationships:** Trust and respect grow between the mentor and mentee, fostering a positive work environment.
- **Creates a Culture of Growth:** Mentorship inspires other team members to seek and offer support, contributing to a collaborative and learning-focused culture.
- **Drives Organizational Success:** As mentees grow, they become more confident, capable, and aligned with organizational goals.

Implementing Mentorship in Leadership

To effectively mentor staff members, leaders must:

1. **Commit to the Process:** Mentorship requires time, patience, and consistency. Leaders must prioritize regular interactions and invest in their mentee's growth.
2. **Set Clear Expectations:** Both the mentor and mentee should understand the purpose of the relationship, goals to work toward, and how progress will be measured.
3. **Tailor the Approach:** Every individual is unique, so mentorship should be personalized to address the specific needs, strengths, and barriers of the staff member.

4. **Model the Behavior:** Leaders must demonstrate the values, attitudes, and work ethic they want to inspire in their mentees.

Addressing Barriers Through Mentorship

Mentorship can effectively address the four common barriers that staff members face:

- **Skill Barriers:** Provide targeted advice, resources, and opportunities for practice.
- **Will Barriers:** Reignite motivation by connecting the mentee's role to the organization's vision and celebrating their progress.
- **Knowledge Barriers:** Share expertise and guide the mentee in acquiring new knowledge or understanding.
- **Capacity Barriers:** Help the mentee prioritize tasks, manage time, and find solutions to reduce overwhelm.

Final Thoughts

> Mentorship is a powerful coaching strategy that goes beyond solving immediate problems; it equips staff members with the tools, confidence, and inspiration to thrive. By sharing experiences, offering feedback, and providing motivation, leaders can transform barriers into opportunities for growth. In doing so, they not only support individual success but also strengthen the entire organization, fostering a culture of development and resilience.

CHAPTER 9

The Suggestions Strategy as a Coach

Effective leadership in a coaching role often relies on providing suggestions that help staff members make meaningful adjustments to overcome barriers to success. Suggestions are not about issuing commands or demands; rather, they represent thoughtful, constructive recommendations that empower staff members to grow, improve, and find solutions. When delivered effectively, suggestions can inspire change, build trust, and lead to lasting improvements in performance.

The Power of Suggestions

Suggestions are a subtle yet powerful tool in the coaching process. Unlike directives, which are firm instructions, suggestions encourage staff members to reflect, evaluate, and decide on a course of action. By giving staff the space to process feedback and implement changes on their own terms, leaders can foster greater ownership, accountability, and motivation.

The key to effective suggestions lies in the balance of clarity and respect. Leaders should offer clear, actionable ideas while also showing respect for the individual's ability to adapt and problem-solve. A well-timed suggestion can act as a catalyst for progress, sparking a shift in behavior or mindset that enables staff to move past their barriers.

When to Offer Suggestions

Suggestions should be given during dedicated coaching sessions when staff members are experiencing challenges or barriers to success. These coaching sessions create a safe and focused space for leaders to:

- Discuss observed struggles or areas of concern.
- Share constructive feedback.
- Collaborate on solutions.
- Encourage staff to reflect on their own progress and needs.

Leaders should avoid offering unsolicited or poorly timed suggestions, as they may be perceived as criticism or micromanagement. Instead, frame suggestions as opportunities for growth, delivered in a supportive and forward-looking manner.

Crafting Effective Suggestions

The impact of a suggestion depends not only on what is said but also on how it is communicated. Effective suggestions are:

1. **Specific and Actionable**

    Vague suggestions can create confusion and frustration. Leaders must be clear about what changes they are recommending and provide specific examples or steps that the staff member can follow.

    Example: *Instead of: "You need to improve your teamwork," try: "During our meetings, I'd like to see you ask for input from your teammates before making decisions. This will help build collaboration."*

2. **Rooted in Observation**

    Suggestions should be based on observable behaviors or situations, not assumptions. Leaders must approach suggestions with facts and context to ensure they are constructive and fair.

    Example: *"I noticed that your project deadlines have been slipping. It might help to break the project into smaller milestones and check progress weekly. This approach has worked for others on the team."*

3. **Delivered with Empathy**

    A coaching relationship is built on trust, so suggestions should always come from a place of empathy and care. Leaders must communicate that their intention is to help the staff member succeed, not to criticize or highlight flaws.

    Example: *"I understand that managing multiple priorities can feel overwhelming. Would you like to try using a priority list or a tool to organize your tasks? I can help you set it up."*

4. **Aligned with Goals**

    Effective suggestions are tied to the goals of the individual, team, and organization. Leaders should connect suggestions to the bigger picture and emphasize how they support professional growth and organizational success.

    Example: *"Your communication skills are strong, but let's focus on enhancing your public speaking. This will prepare you for bigger opportunities to represent the team during client presentations."*

5. **Framed as Collaborative**

    Instead of presenting suggestions as demands, leaders should frame them as collaborative efforts. Involving staff in the discussion about possible solutions encourages buy-in and engagement.

    Example: *"I think adjusting your approach to project*

planning could make a big difference. What are your thoughts on trying a weekly check-in to review progress?"

Suggestions in Action

Consider the following scenario: A staff member is struggling to meet deadlines and feels overwhelmed by their workload. In a coaching session, a leader might say:

> *"I can see you're working hard, but I've noticed that the last few projects have missed their deadlines. I've experienced similar challenges myself in the past. What helped me was breaking down projects into smaller tasks with clear milestones. How would you feel about trying that approach? We can set up a plan together and adjust it as needed."*

In this example, the leader:

- Acknowledges the staff member's effort.
- Identifies the problem without judgment.
- Shares a suggestion rooted in their own experience.
- Invites collaboration and leaves room for the staff member to contribute.

This approach creates a supportive and solutions-focused conversation that empowers the staff member to make changes without feeling criticized.

The Role of Follow-Up

Suggestions are most effective when paired with consistent follow-up. Leaders should check in after coaching sessions to see how the staff member is progressing and offer further support if needed. Follow-up demonstrates that the leader is invested in the staff member's success and provides accountability for implementing the suggested changes.

- **Reinforce Progress:** Acknowledge any improvements or efforts made since the last conversation.
- **Adjust as Needed:** If the suggestion isn't producing results, work together to explore alternative solutions.
- **Offer Continued Support:** Remind the staff member that they are not alone in overcoming their challenges.

Example: *"I've noticed you're making progress on breaking your workload into smaller tasks—well done! How has that been working for you? Are there any areas where you still feel stuck? Let's adjust the plan if needed."*

Final Thoughts

> Suggestions are a vital coaching strategy that can guide staff members through challenges while empowering them to take ownership of their growth. By offering clear, empathetic, and actionable suggestions, leaders create opportunities for improvement without undermining confidence or trust. Coaching sessions become a platform for collaboration, reflection, and forward progress, helping staff overcome barriers and move closer to success.
>
> Effective leaders understand that coaching is not about having all the answers; it's about partnering with staff members to find the right solutions. Suggestions provide the guidance and support needed to make meaningful adjustments, turning challenges into opportunities for growth.

CHAPTER 10

The Modeling Strategy as a Coach

One of the most powerful ways leaders can inspire and support staff members experiencing barriers to success is through modeling. Modeling involves demonstrating the behaviors, attitudes, and performance standards expected of the team. By showing, rather than just telling, leaders provide a concrete example of what success looks like and establish credibility through their actions.

The Role of Modeling in Leadership

Modeling serves as a real-time, practical example for staff members who may struggle to translate abstract concepts or directives into actionable steps. It allows leaders to communicate expectations clearly and provide tangible proof that success is attainable. More than that, modeling creates trust and respect, as staff members see their leaders practicing what they preach.

Modeling also reinforces the organization's values and vision by embedding them into daily actions. A leader who models perseverance, collaboration, and excellence inspires the same in their team, fostering a culture of accountability and growth.

Why Modeling Matters for Struggling Staff Members

For staff members encountering barriers, whether related to skills, knowledge, will, or capacity, seeing a leader in action can clarify what's required to overcome challenges. It bridges the gap between theory and practice, making abstract goals more accessible. Modeling motivates staff by:

1. **Building Confidence:** Observing a leader excel in a challenging task demonstrates that success is possible and provides a roadmap for achieving it.
2. **Offering Clarity:** Modeling breaks down complex processes into observable steps, helping staff understand how to approach their own challenges.
3. **Establishing Trust:** When leaders model desired behaviors, they show that they're willing to hold themselves to the same standards they set for their team.

How to Model Effectively

To make modeling an impactful coaching strategy, leaders must:

1. **Be Intentional**

   Modeling should be purposeful and tailored to the specific barriers a staff member is experiencing. Leaders should identify what behaviors or actions need to be demonstrated and ensure their efforts align with the staff member's goals.

   Example: *If a staff member struggles with time management, the leader might model effective prioritization by openly sharing their daily planning process and tools.*

2. **Showcase Excellence**

   Leaders must strive to deliver exemplary results when modeling. By setting a high standard, they provide staff with an aspirational example to follow. Example: *A leader working alongside their team on a tight deadline demonstrates focus, organization, and a commitment to quality, illustrating how to balance speed with accuracy.*

3. **Be Transparent**

   Modeling isn't just about showing successes; it's also about sharing challenges and strategies for overcoming them. Leaders who admit mistakes and explain how they learned from them make the process more relatable and human.

Example: *A leader might say, "I used to struggle with public speaking too, but I practiced by presenting to small groups first. Let's work on building your confidence step by step."*

4. **Engage in Real-Time Demonstrations**

   Whenever possible, leaders should model behaviors and skills in real-world situations. This makes the learning experience more dynamic and impactful. Example: *During a team meeting, a leader models effective communication by actively listening, asking thoughtful questions, and summarizing key points to ensure clarity.*

5. **Follow Up with Guidance**

   After modeling a behavior or skill, leaders should check in with staff to discuss what they observed, answer questions, and provide additional support.

Modeling in Action

Consider a staff member who is struggling with conflict resolution. A leader might model the desired approach by:

- Facilitating a conversation between two team members with differing perspectives.
- Demonstrating active listening, empathy, and a focus on solutions.

- Explaining their thought process afterward to help the staff member understand the steps involved.

The staff member not only gains insight into effective conflict resolution but also sees how the leader's actions align with the organization's values of respect and collaboration.

Final Thoughts

> Modeling is more than a strategy; it's a commitment to leading by example. By demonstrating the behaviors and skills they want to see in their team, leaders bridge the gap between expectation and execution, inspiring staff to overcome barriers and achieve their potential. When leaders model excellence, they cultivate a culture of integrity, accountability, and continuous improvement, paving the way for individual and organizational success.

CHAPTER 11

The Observation Strategy as a Coach

Observations are one of the most effective tools in a leader's coaching toolkit. When used thoughtfully, they allow leaders to collect valuable data about their team members, identify patterns, and provide objective, actionable feedback. For staff members facing barriers to success, observations offer insights that can illuminate the root causes of challenges and guide tailored interventions.

The Role of Observations in Leadership

Observations serve as a foundation for understanding behavior, performance, and potential. By watching team members in action, leaders gather real-time information about their strengths, weaknesses, and how they respond to various situations. Observations can reveal gaps in skills, knowledge, or motivation that may not be evident through conversation alone.

Unlike assumptions or anecdotal evidence, observations are grounded in facts. This objectivity is crucial for building trust, as it ensures that feedback is fair and accurate. Leaders who base their coaching strategies on direct observations demonstrate a commitment to understanding their team members' unique challenges and opportunities.

Observing to Collect Data

The primary purpose of observations is to collect data that informs coaching decisions. Leaders should approach this process with curiosity and an open mind, seeking to understand rather than to judge. Key elements of effective data collection include:

1. **Preparation**: Determine what you want to observe and why. Are you looking at specific behaviors, interactions, or outcomes? Set clear objectives for your observation to ensure it is focused and purposeful.
2. **Neutrality**: Adopt an unbiased perspective during observations. Avoid interpreting actions or assigning meaning in the moment. Instead, focus on recording what you see and hear without adding assumptions.
3. **Context**: Observe staff members in various settings to gain a well-rounded understanding of their performance. This might include meetings, one-on-one interactions, or task execution.
4. **Detail**: Take thorough notes, capturing both the actions and the context in which they occur. Specific examples

will be invaluable when providing feedback or identifying trends.

One particularly effective practice for capturing detail is **taking a running record**. A running record is a tool that involves documenting word-for-word dialogue and actions during an observation. This method allows leaders to collect highly accurate and detailed information that can be reviewed later for analysis and feedback. Running records are especially helpful when observing communication, instructional techniques, or interactions between team members. By capturing the exact language and behaviors of staff members, leaders can identify patterns, pinpoint misunderstandings, and provide specific, actionable feedback.

Staying Objective

Objectivity is critical to the success of observations. Leaders must separate facts from interpretations to avoid misunderstandings or unfair conclusions. For example:

- **Subjective**: "She doesn't care about the project because she arrived late to the meeting."
- **Objective**: "She arrived 15 minutes late to the meeting without providing an explanation."

By focusing on observable actions rather than assumptions, leaders can maintain credibility and foster trust with their team. Objectivity also ensures that feedback is constructive and actionable, rather than personal or accusatory.

Providing Feedback Based on Observations

Once observations are complete, the next step is to translate them into meaningful feedback. This feedback should be:

1. **Specific**: Use concrete examples from your observations to illustrate your points. Avoid vague statements that leave room for misinterpretation.
   Example:
   - Instead of: "You need to improve your communication."
   - Try: "During yesterday's meeting, I noticed that you didn't ask for input from your teammates. Let's work on creating more opportunities for collaboration."
2. **Balanced**: Highlight both strengths and areas for improvement. Positive reinforcement builds confidence and motivation, while constructive feedback provides clear opportunities for growth.

Example:
- "I was impressed by how you managed the client's questions during the presentation. One area we can work on is incorporating more data to back up your points."

3. **Collaborative**: Frame feedback as a conversation rather than a critique. Invite the staff member to share their perspective and collaborate on solutions.

Example:
- "I've observed that deadlines have been a challenge recently. What do you think is contributing to that, and how can I support you in staying on track?"

Using Observations to Overcome Barriers

Observations are particularly effective when staff members are experiencing barriers to success. By identifying specific behaviors or patterns, leaders can tailor their coaching strategies to address the root causes of challenges. For example:

- **Skill Barriers**: Observations may reveal gaps in technical abilities or processes. Leaders can use this data to recommend training, mentoring, or hands-on practice.
  - Observation: A staff member struggles to use new software effectively.

- Feedback: "I noticed you had difficulty navigating the reporting feature. Let's schedule a training session to build your confidence with the tool."
- **Will Barriers**: Observations may uncover disengagement or resistance to tasks. Leaders can address these issues by exploring underlying motivations and creating opportunities for alignment.
   - Observation: A staff member frequently avoids participating in team discussions.
   - Feedback: "I've noticed you've been quiet during meetings. Is there something on your mind? Let's work on ways to ensure your voice is heard."
- **Knowledge Barriers**: Observations can identify misunderstandings or gaps in information. Leaders can use this insight to clarify expectations or provide additional resources.
   - Observation: A staff member misinterprets instructions and delivers an incomplete task.
   - Feedback: "I saw that the report was missing some key data points. Let's review the instructions together to make sure everything is clear."
- **Capacity Barriers**: Observations may highlight workload imbalances or time management issues. Leaders can address these by reallocating tasks or providing support.

- Observation: A staff member appears overwhelmed and misses multiple deadlines.
- Feedback: "I've noticed that your workload seems heavy. Let's prioritize your tasks and see what we can delegate or adjust."

Building Trust Through Observations

When conducted with care and respect, observations can strengthen the leader-staff relationship. By taking the time to understand individual challenges and provide thoughtful feedback, leaders demonstrate their commitment to supporting their team members' success. Transparency is key—staff should always know that observations are intended to help, not to criticize or micromanage.

Final Thoughts

> Observations are a cornerstone of effective coaching. By remaining objective, focused, and supportive, leaders can gain invaluable insights into their team members' performance and potential. This data serves as the foundation for constructive feedback and targeted interventions that address barriers to success.
>
> Ultimately, observations are not about catching mistakes but about identifying opportunities for growth. When leaders approach this strategy with empathy and intentionality, they create a culture of trust, accountability, and continuous improvement. Through the power of observations, leaders can guide their teams to greater clarity, confidence, and success.

CHAPTER 12

Acknowledgement as a Leadership Strategy for Capacity Barriers

When staff members face capacity barriers to success, the leader's role extends beyond logistical support or task delegation. A critical yet often overlooked strategy is acknowledgement. Recognizing the effort and dedication of team members not only boosts morale but also reinforces a culture of appreciation and respect. By acknowledging contributions—even when challenges remain—leaders can motivate and encourage staff to stay engaged and focused.

The Importance of Acknowledgement

Capacity barriers often arise when staff members are stretched too thin, whether due to high workloads, tight deadlines, or limited resources. These challenges can lead to frustration, burnout, or a sense of being undervalued. In such situations, leaders must step in to affirm the hard work being done and show that their efforts are recognized and appreciated. Acknowledgement fosters a sense of belonging and reminds team members that their contributions matter, even when circumstances are less than ideal.

Forms of Acknowledgement

Acknowledgement can take many forms, ranging from personal notes to public praise. The key is to ensure that the recognition is sincere, specific, and timely. Below are two impactful methods:

1. **Public Praise** Publicly recognizing a team member's efforts during meetings or through organizational communication channels can have a powerful effect. It highlights their achievements to peers and leadership, reinforcing their value to the team. For example:
   - A leader might say during a team meeting: "I want to take a moment to recognize [Name] for stepping up during a particularly demanding week. Your attention to detail and commitment ensured the project stayed on track, and we're grateful for your effort."
   - Use organizational newsletters, emails, or social media platforms to highlight individual or team accomplishments. This not only boosts the morale of the individual being recognized but also sets a positive example for the broader team.
2. **Thank You Notes** A personal thank-you note—either handwritten or digital—can have a lasting impact. It's a simple yet meaningful way to convey appreciation and

connect with team members on a more personal level. Effective thank-you notes should:
- Be specific: Highlight the particular actions or qualities you are acknowledging.
- Be timely: Send the note shortly after the effort or achievement has occurred.
- Reflect authenticity: Use genuine language that conveys sincerity and gratitude.

3. Example:
   - "Dear [Name], I wanted to personally thank you for the incredible effort you put into [specific task or project]. Despite the heavy workload, you managed to deliver exceptional results, and I truly appreciate your dedication and professionalism. You're an invaluable part of our team."

How Acknowledgement Addresses Capacity Barriers

Acknowledgement addresses capacity barriers by validating the efforts of team members who may feel overwhelmed or underappreciated. It reminds them that their hard work does not go unnoticed and that the organization values their contributions. This can help:

- **Boost morale**: Recognition inspires motivation and a renewed sense of purpose.
- **Strengthen resilience**: Acknowledged team members are more likely to persevere through challenges.
- **Foster loyalty**: Employees who feel valued are more likely to stay engaged and committed to the organization.

Best Practices for Effective Acknowledgement

While acknowledgement is a powerful tool, it must be done thoughtfully to achieve its intended impact. Consider the following best practices:

1. **Be Specific**: Generic praise can feel insincere. Instead, focus on specific actions or outcomes that demonstrate the individual's contributions.
2. **Be Consistent**: Make recognition a regular practice rather than an occasional gesture.
3. **Be Inclusive**: Ensure that all team members receive acknowledgement for their efforts, not just high performers or those in visible roles.
4. **Be Authentic**: Avoid exaggerated praise or empty compliments. Genuine appreciation resonates more deeply.

Balancing Acknowledgement with Capacity Management

While acknowledgement is essential, it should complement—not replace—practical strategies to address capacity barriers. Leaders must also:

- Assess workloads and redistribute tasks as needed.
- Advocate for additional resources or support to alleviate pressure.
- Provide tools and training to improve efficiency and reduce strain.

Acknowledgement works best when paired with actionable steps to address the root causes of capacity barriers. This holistic approach demonstrates that leaders not only value their team's efforts but are also committed to their well-being and success.

Final Thoughts

> Acknowledgement is a simple yet profound way to support staff members facing capacity barriers. By recognizing their contributions through public praise, thank-you notes, or other means, leaders can boost morale, build trust, and foster a culture of appreciation. When combined with practical strategies to manage workloads and resources, acknowledgement becomes a cornerstone of effective leadership—one that inspires teams to overcome challenges and achieve their best.

CHAPTER 13

Grace as a Leadership Strategy for Capacity Barriers

In the fast-paced and demanding environment of today's organizations, staff members will inevitably encounter periods when their capacity to perform is stretched to its limits. While holding staff accountable for results remains essential, effective leaders understand that sometimes the most impactful strategy is extending grace. Grace is not about lowering expectations or excusing poor performance—it is about recognizing human limitations, offering support, and providing the space and time needed to overcome capacity barriers.

Leaders who extend grace demonstrate empathy, build trust, and foster an environment where staff feel supported rather than judged during difficult times. It is a strategy that provides the emotional and practical support necessary for staff members to regain balance, recover, and ultimately succeed.

The Meaning of Grace in Leadership

Grace in leadership is about showing understanding and flexibility when a team member faces capacity challenges. Capacity barriers can arise from personal circumstances, overwhelming workloads, unexpected changes, or resource limitations. Leaders who extend grace acknowledge that people are not machines—they need time, space, and support to navigate such challenges.

Extending grace involves:

- Offering **extended time** to complete tasks or meet expectations.
- Creating **more space** by temporarily relieving certain responsibilities or redistributing workload.
- Providing **additional opportunities** to improve performance or develop skills without immediate repercussions.

Grace, when applied appropriately, sends a powerful message: "I see your struggle, I believe in your ability to overcome it, and I'm here to support you."

Strategies for Extending Grace

Leaders can employ various methods to extend grace to team members facing capacity barriers while maintaining accountability and organizational performance.

1. **Offering Extended Time** When a staff member is overwhelmed or struggling to meet deadlines, providing additional time can alleviate immediate pressure and allow them to focus on delivering quality work.
   - Example: "I know you've been balancing multiple priorities, and this project has been a heavy lift. I'm extending the deadline by three days so you can finalize it without rushing."
2. Leaders must communicate that extended time is not about lowering expectations but about creating the conditions for success. Deadlines remain important, but flexibility during challenging moments can make the difference between failure and achievement.
3. **Creating Space** Sometimes staff members need space to reset and recover. This may involve temporarily adjusting workloads, reassigning tasks, or allowing time for personal obligations to be managed without fear of judgment.
   - Example: A leader may step in and say, "I've noticed you've been working long hours on multiple projects.

Let's redistribute some tasks so you can focus on the highest priorities and find a better balance."
4. By creating space, leaders give their team the mental clarity and emotional bandwidth needed to tackle challenges effectively.
5. **Providing Additional Opportunities to Improve** Grace also involves offering staff members multiple opportunities to improve performance when they fall short. Leaders can frame these opportunities as learning experiences rather than failures, motivating staff to rise to the challenge.
    - Example: "The last presentation didn't fully meet the goals we discussed, but I know you're capable of doing great work. Let's review the feedback together and create a plan for success on the next one."
6. Providing additional opportunities reinforces the leader's belief in the staff member's potential and creates an environment where failure is seen as a stepping stone to growth.

A Real-World Example of Grace in Action

Consider a scenario where a high-performing team member begins to miss deadlines and deliver incomplete work. Rather than immediately reprimanding them, the leader schedules a private conversation to better understand the situation. During the discussion, the staff member reveals they have been struggling to balance a demanding workload with personal family obligations.

The leader extends grace by:

- Temporarily shifting non-critical tasks to other team members.
- Adjusting the timeline on a major project to allow the staff member to catch up.
- Offering emotional support and affirming their confidence in the staff member's ability to overcome the challenge.

Over the next few weeks, the staff member regains focus and begins to deliver high-quality work. By extending grace instead of reacting punitively, the leader preserved the staff member's morale and prevented burnout while ensuring success was ultimately achieved.

The Impact of Grace on Teams

Extending grace has a profound and lasting impact on teams and organizational culture. When leaders demonstrate understanding and flexibility during difficult times:

- **Trust deepens**: Staff members feel safe acknowledging challenges without fear of harsh judgment or repercussions.
- **Loyalty increases**: Employees are more likely to remain committed to leaders who treat them with compassion and fairness.
- **Performance improves**: Grace provides the breathing room staff need to reset and return to delivering their best work.
- **Resilience builds**: Teams develop a culture where mistakes and setbacks are seen as opportunities to learn and improve rather than as failures.

However, it is important for leaders to ensure that grace is not misinterpreted as an excuse for complacency. Extending grace requires balance—it is about offering support and space while maintaining clear expectations for improvement.

Best Practices for Extending Grace

To effectively use grace as a leadership strategy, consider the following best practices:

1. **Know Your Team**: Understanding each team member's capacity, strengths, and challenges allows leaders to extend grace in a way that is tailored and meaningful.
2. **Communicate Clearly**: Clearly articulate expectations, adjustments, and timelines when offering grace to avoid misunderstandings.
3. **Document Adjustments**: When extending grace in the form of time or space, document these changes to ensure alignment and fairness.
4. **Follow Up**: Check in with team members to assess progress and provide additional support as needed.
5. **Be Consistent**: Apply grace equitably to prevent perceptions of favoritism.

Final Thoughts

> Grace is a powerful leadership strategy that allows staff members to overcome capacity barriers without fear of judgment or failure. By offering extended time, creating space, and providing additional opportunities to improve, leaders empower their teams to navigate challenges while reinforcing trust and commitment.
>
> Leadership is about balancing accountability with compassion. Extending grace does not mean lowering standards; it means helping team members achieve those standards through understanding and support. When leaders embrace grace as part of their approach, they cultivate resilient, motivated, and high-performing teams capable of overcoming even the most difficult challenges.

CHAPTER 14

Scheduled Check-Ins as a Leadership Strategy for Capacity Barriers

When staff members face capacity barriers that prevent them from performing at their best, effective leaders recognize the importance of ongoing, intentional communication. Scheduled check-ins serve as a vital leadership strategy to address these barriers by creating dedicated time to connect, follow up, and offer targeted support. Unlike reactive or sporadic conversations, scheduled check-ins are intentional, structured, and personalized to the needs of the struggling staff member.

The Purpose of Scheduled Check-Ins

Scheduled check-ins are designed to provide struggling staff members with a consistent opportunity to share concerns, discuss challenges, and receive support from their leader. These one-on-one meetings are more than a simple conversation; they are a proactive leadership tool that fosters trust, reinforces accountability, and demonstrates genuine care for the individual's well-being and success.

At their core, scheduled check-ins serve three primary purposes:

1. **Follow-Up**: Leaders revisit concerns or situations discussed in prior conversations, ensuring progress is being made and barriers are being addressed.
2. **Support**: Leaders provide guidance, encouragement, and solutions for capacity challenges, whether professional or personal.
3. **Reinforcement**: Leaders use these opportunities to communicate expectations, priorities, and the belief that improvement is both possible and attainable.

Structure of Effective Scheduled Check-Ins

To make scheduled check-ins impactful, leaders must approach them with intention and consistency. Below are key components of an effective check-in:

1. **Schedule a Convenient Time** Check-ins must be scheduled at a time that works for both the leader and the staff member. For staff members facing capacity barriers, timing is critical. Leaders must demonstrate sensitivity to the individual's workload, stress levels, and personal situation.

- Example: A leader might say, "I'd like to meet with you for 30 minutes this Friday to discuss how things are going. Is there a time that works best for you?"

2. **Begin with Open Communication** Start the meeting by creating a safe space for the staff member to share their current experiences and struggles. Active listening is essential here—leaders must be fully present and engaged to understand the nuances of the situation.
    - Example: "How have things been going since our last meeting? Are there any challenges that have come up recently?"

3. **Follow Up on Previous Concerns** Leaders should revisit prior conversations to assess progress or address ongoing challenges. This reinforces accountability while showing that the leader genuinely cares about the individual's situation and success.
    - Example: "Last time we talked, you mentioned you were struggling with balancing the new project alongside your regular workload. How has that been going? Have the adjustments we discussed helped?"

4. **Provide Feedback and Solutions** Leaders can use check-ins as an opportunity to provide constructive feedback, brainstorm solutions, and offer additional resources or support where necessary.

- Example: "It sounds like you're still feeling overwhelmed by the timeline. Would it help if we adjusted the project deadlines, or redistributed part of the workload for now?"

5. **Address Personal Barriers with Empathy** Sometimes capacity barriers stem from personal circumstances outside of work. While leaders must maintain appropriate boundaries, they should acknowledge personal challenges and offer grace, understanding, and flexibility.
    - Example: "You shared last week that you're dealing with some family obligations that have been taking up a lot of your time. I appreciate you being open about that. How can I best support you right now?"

6. **Conclude with Clear Next Steps** Leaders should wrap up the meeting with clear takeaways, including agreed-upon action items, timelines, and the next scheduled check-in.
    - Example: "Here's what we'll do moving forward: I'll connect with [team member] to help with part of the workload, and you can focus on finishing the presentation by next Thursday. Let's check in again next Friday to see how things are progressing."

Benefits of Scheduled Check-Ins

When done effectively, scheduled check-ins can make a significant difference in helping staff overcome capacity barriers. The benefits include:

1. **Rebuilding Trust and Connection** Regular check-ins demonstrate that leaders are invested in their staff's success, which builds trust and strengthens relationships.
2. **Early Identification of Issues** By consistently following up, leaders can identify issues before they escalate, allowing for early intervention and support.
3. **Providing Emotional Support** For staff members struggling with personal or professional barriers, scheduled check-ins serve as a reminder that they are not alone and that their leader cares about their well-being.
4. **Improving Accountability** Scheduled check-ins establish a routine of accountability without creating a punitive environment. Staff members know they have regular opportunities to communicate progress and challenges.
5. **Boosting Confidence and Motivation** Regular communication and follow-up reinforce the leader's belief in the staff member's ability to overcome barriers, motivating them to keep pushing forward.

A Real-World Example of Scheduled Check-Ins in Action

Consider a staff member named Sarah who has been struggling to keep up with deadlines due to personal challenges at home. Her leader, recognizing Sarah's capacity barrier, schedules weekly check-ins to provide consistent support.

During these meetings, the leader:

- Creates a safe space for Sarah to share her struggles without judgment.
- Revisits prior concerns and assesses whether suggested solutions have been effective.
- Adjusts workloads and deadlines as needed to reduce pressure.
- Provides Sarah with reassurance, guidance, and encouragement to keep moving forward.

Over time, Sarah begins to regain confidence, improve her productivity, and manage her responsibilities more effectively. The scheduled check-ins become a critical support system, allowing Sarah to successfully navigate her challenges.

Final Thoughts

Scheduled check-ins are a powerful and compassionate leadership strategy for supporting staff members facing capacity barriers. By offering regular, structured opportunities to connect, leaders can follow up on challenges, address personal or professional barriers, and provide the necessary guidance and support. These one-on-one conversations build trust, foster accountability, and create an environment where staff members feel seen, heard, and valued.

Leadership requires both presence and intentionality—scheduled check-ins embody both. Through consistent communication and follow-up, leaders empower their staff to overcome capacity challenges and achieve success, one conversation at a time.

CHAPTER 15

Providing Professional Development as a Leadership Strategy for Knowledge Barriers

When staff members face knowledge barriers that prevent them from achieving success, leaders must recognize the importance of growth and learning as part of their coaching strategy. Professional development is an effective and targeted approach that empowers staff to acquire the skills, tools, and understanding needed to overcome knowledge gaps and perform at higher levels.

Professional development is not a one-size-fits-all solution; it must be intentional, tailored to individual needs, and aligned with the organization's goals. By investing in staff learning, leaders demonstrate their commitment to both individual and organizational success while fostering a culture of continuous improvement.

Understanding Professional Development

Professional development is a structured process of building knowledge and expertise through learning opportunities. It can take many forms—formal or informal, virtual or in-person, delivered internally or externally—and is always aimed at improving job performance and overall capacity.

The key components of professional development include:

- **Targeted Learning**: Addressing specific knowledge gaps or skill deficiencies identified during coaching or supervisory sessions.
- **Purpose-Driven Content**: Aligning professional development opportunities with organizational goals, team priorities, and individual growth needs.
- **Ongoing Application**: Ensuring staff can apply what they learn directly to their roles, creating measurable results.

Professional development is more than attending training sessions or conferences—it is a strategy for building confidence, competence, and long-term success.

Types of Professional Development

Leaders can use a variety of professional development opportunities to address knowledge barriers. The key is choosing the format and approach that best fits the needs of the staff member and the context of their role.

1. **Virtual Professional Development** Online platforms, webinars, and virtual courses offer flexibility and accessibility, making professional development achievable even in a busy work environment. Leaders can identify targeted courses or resources that staff members can complete at their own pace.
   - Example: "I've noticed you're struggling with the new software tools. Let's enroll you in a virtual training program that provides step-by-step tutorials. It will give you the confidence to use the platform effectively."
2. **In-Person Training and Workshops** In-person professional development, such as workshops, seminars, or training sessions, allows for hands-on learning, interaction, and direct feedback. Leaders can identify external opportunities or organize internal sessions.
   - Example: "There's a leadership workshop happening next month that focuses on communication skills. I think it would be a great opportunity for you to sharpen your presentation abilities."
3. **Offsite Professional Development** Offsite opportunities, like conferences or industry events, expose staff to new ideas, emerging trends, and best practices within their field. These experiences often re-energize staff

members by connecting them with professionals who share similar challenges.
- Example: "Attending this annual conference will allow you to learn from experts in the field and bring back strategies we can apply to our team's projects."

4. **Peer-to-Peer Learning** Sometimes, professional development comes from within the organization. Leaders can leverage the skills and expertise of team members who have demonstrated success in a particular area. Peer-to-peer training fosters collaboration and allows staff to learn from real-world experiences.
    - Example: "Since Alex has had great success in managing client accounts, I've asked him to host a session to share his strategies with the team."

Strategies for Implementing Professional Development

To make professional development impactful, leaders must approach it with intention and clear goals. Below are strategies to implement professional development effectively:

1. **Identify Knowledge Gaps** Professional development should directly address the knowledge or skill deficiencies preventing a staff member from achieving success.

Leaders can identify gaps through observations, coaching conversations, or performance reviews.
- Example: "I've noticed there are some challenges in understanding the new project management system. Let's find training that focuses on this specific tool."

2. **Set Clear Learning Objectives** Before engaging in professional development, leaders must set clear expectations for what the staff member will gain from the experience. This helps ensure alignment with organizational needs.
   - Example: "The goal of attending this seminar is for you to learn advanced budgeting techniques that we can implement in next quarter's planning process."

3. **Provide Time and Support** Leaders must create space for staff to fully engage with professional development opportunities. This includes offering flexibility in schedules and workloads to prioritize learning.
   - Example: "Take the afternoon to focus on this virtual training module, and let's meet next week to discuss what you learned and how it applies to your role."

4. **Follow Up and Apply Learning** After professional development, leaders should follow up with the staff member to assess their learning and identify opportunities to apply new skills. This reinforces accountability and ensures knowledge translates into action.

- Example: "What were the key takeaways from the workshop? Let's create a plan to incorporate these strategies into your daily workflow."
5. **Celebrate Growth and Success** Acknowledge the effort and progress made through professional development. Celebrating growth motivates staff to continue learning and improving.
    - Example: "Your ability to analyze data has improved significantly since completing the training. I can see the impact in your recent reports—great work!"

The Role of Leaders in Professional Development

Leaders play a critical role in guiding, supporting, and encouraging professional development for staff members experiencing knowledge barriers. Their responsibilities include:

- **Identifying opportunities**: Proactively seeking professional development resources that address team needs.
- **Advocating for learning**: Promoting a culture where ongoing development is valued and prioritized.
- **Removing barriers**: Ensuring staff have the time, resources, and support to engage fully in professional development.

- **Modeling growth**: Demonstrating a commitment to learning by participating in professional development themselves.

By actively supporting professional development, leaders empower their staff to build the knowledge and skills needed to excel, innovate, and contribute meaningfully to the organization.

A Real-World Example of Professional Development in Action

Consider a staff member named John who struggles with delivering effective presentations. His leader identifies this as a knowledge barrier and recommends targeted professional development:

1. The leader enrolls John in a virtual course on public speaking techniques.
2. John attends an offsite workshop that allows him to practice speaking skills in front of a small audience.
3. A peer on the team who excels at presentations shares their tips and experiences during a one-on-one coaching session.

Through these targeted professional development opportunities, John gains confidence and mastery over his presentation skills. His next presentation is delivered with clarity, impact, and professionalism—demonstrating how effective professional development can turn knowledge barriers into opportunities for growth.

Final Thoughts

> Professional development is one of the most powerful tools leaders have for addressing knowledge barriers and fostering individual and organizational growth. By offering targeted, purpose-driven learning opportunities—whether virtual, in-person, or peer-led—leaders demonstrate their commitment to staff success.
>
> Investing in professional development creates a culture where continuous learning is celebrated, staff are empowered to reach their full potential, and knowledge barriers are transformed into pathways to excellence. Leadership is not just about recognizing challenges but equipping others with the tools, experiences, and opportunities needed to overcome them.

CHAPTER 16

Providing Resources as a Leadership Strategy for Knowledge Barriers

When staff members encounter knowledge barriers, one of the most effective strategies a leader can use is providing targeted resources to bridge the gap. Knowledge gaps often stem from a lack of exposure, education, or understanding, and these barriers can impede growth, confidence, and performance. Providing resources such as videos, articles, books, and tools enables staff to gain new knowledge, develop their skills, and move toward success.

Resources offer a foundation for learning by giving staff access to concrete information, examples, and insights that directly address their areas of struggle. As a leader, the act of supplying resources demonstrates an investment in the individual's development while empowering them to take ownership of their learning journey. However, it is essential to note that providing resources is not meant to replace actual leader support. Resources should supplement the leader's ongoing coaching, mentorship, and guidance—not serve as a substitute for it.

Understanding the Role of Resources

Resources are tools designed to support learning and improvement. They can come in many forms, but their purpose is consistent: to provide staff with the knowledge they need to overcome barriers and succeed. Unlike professional development, which often requires time, structure, and larger-scale commitments, resources are usually more accessible and flexible. Leaders can provide targeted resources tailored to specific issues, making it a practical and immediate solution.

By offering resources, leaders help staff:

- **Build knowledge and skills** in targeted areas.
- **Work at their own pace** to process and implement new learning.
- **Gain clarity** on concepts or processes they find challenging.
- **Feel supported** in a way that reduces frustration and overwhelm.

When used effectively, resources can be the difference between continued struggle and meaningful progress.

Types of Resources Leaders Can Provide

1. **Videos** are a dynamic and engaging way to deliver knowledge. Whether through online tutorials, recorded webinars, or educational content, videos offer step-by-step demonstrations and practical explanations that are easy to follow. Leaders can identify videos that align with the specific knowledge barrier being experienced.
    - *Example*: "I found a short video that walks through the process of using our new project management software. Watch this, and let's touch base afterward to clarify any questions you have."

2. **Articles** are a quick and effective way to deliver concise, targeted information. They can provide fresh insights, expert tips, or strategies that staff can immediately apply to their work. Leaders should curate articles that are clear, relevant, and practical.
    - *Example*: "I came across this article on time management strategies that I think could help you balance your workload. Take a look, and we can discuss how to implement these ideas."

3. **Books** are a powerful resource for deeper learning and long-term growth. They offer detailed information, research-based strategies, and thought-provoking perspectives that staff members can use to expand their

knowledge and mindset. Leaders can recommend books that address both technical skills and professional development topics.
- *Example*: "This book has been instrumental in helping others improve their leadership communication skills. I'd like to give you a copy so you can explore the strategies outlined."

4. **Templates, Tools, and Guides** Providing templates, checklists, or practical tools can simplify processes and give staff clear frameworks to follow. These resources address knowledge gaps by providing step-by-step guidance that reduces ambiguity and increases efficiency.
    - *Example*: "Here's a template for writing project summaries. It includes examples of what a strong summary should look like. Let me know if you need further clarification."

5. **Online Learning Platforms** Leaders can recommend free or paid platforms with courses, lessons, or skill-building modules. Online learning platforms allow staff to explore topics at their own pace while filling knowledge gaps with structured content.
    - *Example*: "There's a course on leadership skills on LinkedIn Learning that would be beneficial for you.

It covers the concepts we've been discussing in our coaching sessions."

How Leaders Provide Resources Effectively

Providing resources isn't just about handing over a video or article and walking away. To make this strategy effective, leaders must:

1. **Identify the Knowledge Barrier** Leaders must first pinpoint the specific knowledge gap. Is it a lack of technical expertise, unfamiliarity with a process, or difficulty understanding a core concept? Observations, coaching conversations, and feedback sessions can help leaders determine where the knowledge barrier exists.
   - *Example*: "I noticed during your last presentation that the data analysis lacked detail. I think there's a gap in understanding how to interpret these metrics."
2. **Curate the Right Resource** Choose resources that directly address the identified barrier. Resources should be clear, relevant, and appropriate to the staff member's learning style and level of understanding.
   - *Example*: "This article breaks down data interpretation in simple terms. I think it will help clarify the concepts you're struggling with."

3. **Discuss and Introduce the Resource** Leaders should introduce the resource thoughtfully, explaining why it's being provided and what the staff member should focus on. This sets expectations and demonstrates the leader's investment in the individual's success.
    - *Example*: "I want you to review this training video because it outlines the key steps for project planning. Pay special attention to how timelines are created."
4. **Follow Up on Progress** Providing a resource is only part of the process. Leaders must follow up to ensure the resource was helpful, clarify any lingering questions, and discuss how to apply the learning.
    - *Example*: "How did you find the article on time management? Were there strategies that you think will work for your schedule? Let's create a plan to try them out this week."
5. **Encourage Ownership of Learning** While leaders provide resources, staff must take ownership of their learning. Leaders can empower staff to engage with the resource, reflect on their growth, and seek additional support if needed.
    - *Example*: "This book is a great starting point, but it's up to you to implement what resonates most. Let's check in next week to see how it's going."

A Real-World Example: Providing Resources for Success

Consider Sarah, a staff member struggling to organize large-scale events. Her leader identifies that Sarah lacks knowledge about effective event planning processes. The leader provides the following resources:

1. A step-by-step video on event planning basics.
2. An article on creating detailed timelines and task lists for events.
3. A guide with templates for budgeting, scheduling, and tracking event logistics.

The leader introduces these resources during a coaching session and follows up with Sarah after a week. By combining accessible tools with ongoing support, Sarah gains the knowledge and confidence needed to plan and execute successful events.

Final Thoughts

> Providing resources is a practical and effective strategy for addressing knowledge barriers. By offering videos, articles, books, tools, and templates, leaders empower staff members to overcome challenges and build essential knowledge. This strategy reflects a leader's commitment to individual growth and organizational success.
>
> It is important to remember that resources are not a replacement for actual leader support. Leaders must remain present and engaged, using resources as a supplement to their guidance, coaching, and mentorship. By thoughtfully curating and following up on resources, leaders create a supportive environment where staff can learn, grow, and ultimately achieve success.

CHAPTER 17

Generational Workplace Values and Characteristics

Workplaces today are often multigenerational, with employees from different generational cohorts working side by side. Each generation brings its own values, characteristics, and expectations, shaped by the unique social, economic, and cultural events they experienced during their formative years. For leaders, understanding these generational differences is essential to fostering collaboration, mutual respect, and productivity in the workplace.

The Generations in the Workplace

Traditionalists (Silent Generation)
- **Birth Years:** 1928–1945
- **Current Age (2024):** 79–96
- **Workplace Values:**
    - Loyalty to the organization.
    - Respect for hierarchy and authority.
    - Hard work and dedication as core principles.

- Preference for stability and tradition.
- **Workplace Characteristics:**
    - Tend to be formal and professional in communication and behavior.
    - Strong emphasis on following rules and protocols.
    - Value face-to-face communication over digital methods.
    - May be less adaptable to rapid technological changes.

Baby Boomers
- **Birth Years:** 1946–1964
- **Current Age (2024):** 60–78
- **Workplace Values:**
    - Strong work ethic and drive for career success.
    - Value job security and steady advancement.
    - Competitive and goal-oriented.
    - Emphasis on team collaboration.
- **Workplace Characteristics:**
    - Prefer structured hierarchies and clear roles.
    - Thrive in environments that reward loyalty and commitment.
    - May resist rapid change but are willing to adapt if given sufficient training.

- Tend to prefer in-person meetings but are increasingly comfortable with technology.

Generation X
- **Birth Years:** 1965–1980
- **Current Age (2024):** 44–59
- **Workplace Values:**
    - Independence and self-reliance.
    - Work-life balance as a priority.
    - Preference for results over process.
    - Skepticism of authority and large institutions.
- **Workplace Characteristics:**
    - Adaptable to both traditional and digital work environments.
    - Prefer flexible work arrangements (e.g., remote work).
    - Tend to focus on efficiency and productivity.
    - Value professional development and lifelong learning opportunities.

Millennials (Generation Y)
- **Birth Years:** 1981–1996
- **Current Age (2024):** 28–43
- **Workplace Values:**

- Desire for meaningful work and purpose-driven careers.
- Emphasis on collaboration and teamwork.
- Value feedback and recognition.
- Seek opportunities for growth and learning.

- **Workplace Characteristics:**
  - Comfortable with technology and digital communication.
  - Thrive in workplaces with mentorship and regular feedback.
  - Advocate for diversity, equity, and inclusion.
  - Flexible in work arrangements but value work-life harmony.

Generation Z

- **Birth Years:** 1997–2012
- **Current Age (2024):** 12–27
- **Workplace Values:**
  - Strong focus on innovation and entrepreneurship.
  - Desire for stability but not at the cost of personal values.
  - Prioritize mental health and well-being.
  - Seek authenticity and transparency from leaders.

- **Workplace Characteristics:**
    - Highly proficient with digital tools and social media.
    - Prefer hybrid or fully remote work environments.
    - Expect frequent communication and clear expectations.
    - Value diversity, inclusion, and social responsibility.

Bridging the Generational Gap

Leaders who understand the values and characteristics of each generation can create inclusive workplaces where everyone feels valued. Here are a few strategies for navigating generational differences:

1. **Encourage Cross-Generational Mentorship**
    - Pair employees from different generations to share knowledge, skills, and perspectives. For example, Baby Boomers can mentor younger employees on institutional knowledge, while Millennials and Gen Z can share insights on technology and innovation.
2. **Customize Communication Styles**
    - Use a mix of communication methods, such as in-person meetings for Traditionalists and Boomers, and digital tools for Millennials and Gen Z. Adapt your tone and delivery based on generational preferences.

3. **Provide Flexible Work Options**
   - Recognize that different generations may have varying needs regarding flexibility. Gen X, Millennials, and Gen Z often prioritize remote work, while Boomers may prefer more structured arrangements.
4. **Foster Inclusive Work Cultures**
   - Create an environment where all generations feel respected and valued. Celebrate generational diversity by recognizing the unique contributions of each cohort.
5. **Offer Tailored Development Opportunities**
   - Provide learning programs that align with the values of each generation. For example, Millennials may prefer collaborative workshops, while Gen X values self-paced, goal-oriented training.

Increasing Collective Efficacy Through Generational Understanding

When leaders acknowledge and respect generational differences, they foster an environment of trust and mutual appreciation. This understanding can:

- **Build Collective Efficacy:**
   - By leveraging the unique strengths of each generation,

leaders create a cohesive team where members trust in each other's capabilities and work toward shared goals.
- For example, combining the experience of Baby Boomers with the tech-savviness of Millennials and Gen Z can result in innovative solutions to complex challenges.

- **Promote Teamwork:**
  - Recognizing generational values encourages collaboration by aligning team dynamics with individual strengths and preferences. For instance, Baby Boomers' focus on teamwork complements Millennials' drive for purpose, leading to meaningful and productive collaborations.

- **Enhance Staff Retention:**
  - Employees who feel understood and valued are more likely to remain loyal to the organization. Providing tailored development opportunities and flexible work arrangements helps meet the diverse needs of a multigenerational workforce.

- **Encourage Development:**
  - When leaders invest in generational-specific strategies like mentorship, professional development, and flexible communication styles, employees feel empowered to grow and succeed within the organization.

Final Thoughts

Generational diversity in the workplace is both a challenge and an opportunity. By understanding the values and characteristics of each generation, leaders can foster a culture of respect, collaboration, and shared success. Recognizing and leveraging the strengths of each cohort ensures that organizations thrive in a rapidly changing world.

Moreover, a leader's ability to integrate these insights into daily practices builds collective efficacy, creates a positive work environment, and enhances staff retention and development. When generational differences are not just acknowledged but celebrated, the workplace becomes a thriving ecosystem of innovation, teamwork, and growth.

CHAPTER 18

Empowering Leadership Through Generational Understanding and Strategies

Leadership is most effective when it aligns with the diverse values and characteristics of the individuals it seeks to guide. The strategies outlined in this book—from delegation and observation to mentorship and grace—become exponentially more impactful when leaders incorporate an understanding of generational differences into their approach. By doing so, leaders can empower their teams, develop individual potential, and foster a culture of collective efficacy.

The Power of Coupling Leadership Strategies with Generational Insights

Each generation brings a unique perspective to the workplace. These perspectives influence how employees approach their roles, interact with peers, and respond to leadership. When leaders consider generational values and characteristics alongside the strategies detailed in this book, they can:

- **Enhance Team Cohesion:** Acknowledging generational differences allows leaders to tailor strategies that promote understanding and collaboration.
- **Empower Individual Success:** Aligning leadership strategies with generational needs helps employees feel valued and supported, leading to higher engagement and performance.
- **Drive Organizational Growth:** When employees from all generations feel understood and aligned with leadership, collective efficacy grows, creating a unified drive toward organizational goals.

Strategies in Action: Bridging Generational Differences

Delegation for Multi-Generational Teams

Delegation is a cornerstone of leadership, but generational differences influence how tasks should be assigned. For example:

- **Baby Boomers (1946–1964):** Appreciate clear instructions and the opportunity to demonstrate their commitment and expertise. Delegating a major project that highlights their skills and organizational knowledge can boost their motivation.

- **Generation X (1965–1980):** Value independence and flexibility. Delegating results-oriented tasks with clear objectives but minimal micromanagement allows them to thrive.
- **Millennials (1981–1996):** Prefer collaborative opportunities and purpose-driven work. Delegating tasks with a social impact or tied to team success can inspire higher engagement.
- **Generation Z (1997–2012):** Look for innovative and technology-driven challenges. Delegating tasks that leverage their digital fluency and creativity ensures they feel relevant and engaged.

By understanding these nuances, leaders can distribute responsibilities in ways that maximize individual strengths and generational preferences.

Mentorship for Growth Across Generations

Mentorship is one of the most powerful coaching strategies a leader can offer. Generational understanding enhances mentorship by enabling leaders to adapt their guidance to resonate with their mentees:

- **Traditionalists (1928–1945):** Share their wealth of experience through storytelling and by highlighting the importance of institutional history. Leaders mentoring Traditionalists should acknowledge their contributions and offer opportunities to impart wisdom to younger generations.
- **Generation X:** Often self-reliant, they respond well to mentors who respect their independence while offering targeted advice for professional development.
- **Millennials:** Seek mentors who provide ongoing feedback, recognition, and career advancement opportunities. Sharing personal experiences and aligning mentorship with their career goals can strengthen the leader-employee relationship.
- **Generation Z:** Desire authenticity and transparency in their mentors. Leaders should focus on creating trust and sharing how their own experiences relate to current trends and challenges.

Acknowledgement and Recognition

Acknowledgement as a strategy resonates universally but has generational-specific impacts:

- **Baby Boomers:** Public praise and formal recognition—such as awards—align with their preference for acknowledgment of loyalty and dedication.
- **Millennials:** Appreciate immediate and informal recognition, such as a quick thank-you note or social media shoutout.
- **Generation Z:** Respond well to personalized recognition that ties their contributions to larger organizational goals or societal impact.

By tailoring acknowledgement efforts to generational values, leaders can reinforce positive behaviors and motivate employees effectively.

Collective Efficacy Through Understanding

When leadership strategies are informed by generational values, they contribute to a culture of collective efficacy—the shared belief in the team's ability to succeed. Leaders can:

1. **Leverage Generational Strengths:** Use the organizational knowledge of Baby Boomers, the adaptability of Generation X, the collaborative mindset of Millennials, and the innovation of Generation Z to create dynamic and high-performing teams.
2. **Promote Mutual Learning:** Encourage cross-generational mentorship, where experienced employees and digital natives exchange skills and knowledge.
3. **Tailor Development Opportunities:** Customize professional development programs to align with generational learning preferences, ensuring all employees feel equipped to succeed.
4. **Foster Inclusion:** Recognize and celebrate generational diversity as an asset. For instance, a leader who understands the work-life balance priorities of Generation X can model flexibility for the entire team, fostering greater trust and respect.

Creating a Positive Work Environment

A leader who integrates generational understanding with strategies such as delegation, observation, and communication can:

- **Promote Teamwork:** By respecting and valuing generational differences, leaders create an environment where employees collaborate effectively.
- **Increase Staff Retention:** Employees are more likely to remain with an organization where their unique needs and contributions are acknowledged.
- **Develop Future Leaders:** Generationally informed strategies prepare employees to step into leadership roles themselves, ensuring organizational sustainability.

Final Thoughts

> Empowering leadership requires both strategic action and emotional intelligence. By combining the strategies in this book with a deep understanding of generational values and characteristics, leaders can create a workplace culture that is inclusive, supportive, and high-performing. The result is not only the development and retention of talented staff but also the cultivation of collective efficacy that drives sustained organizational success.
>
> Leadership is not one-size-fits-all, but when leaders adapt their approach to meet the needs of diverse generations, they embody the true essence of effective and transformative leadership.

EMPOWERING LEADERSHIP THROUGH GENERATIONAL UNDERSTANDING AND STRATEGIES

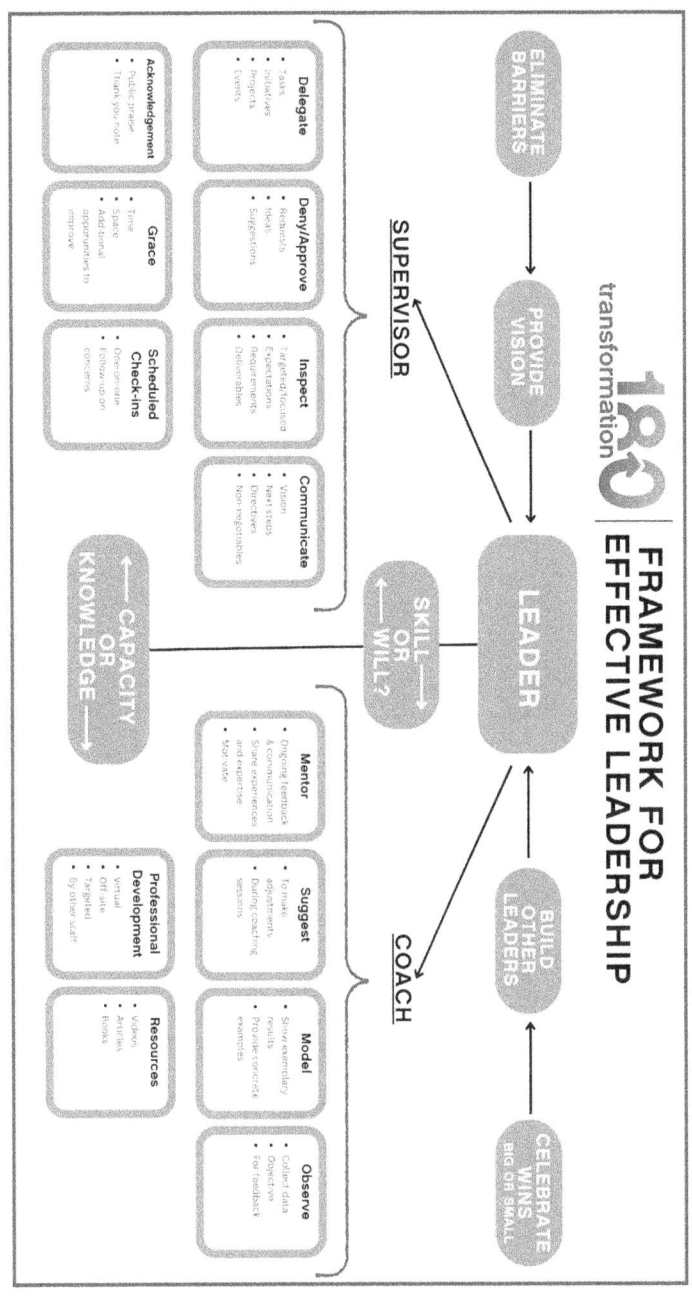

CHAPTER 19

Putting Strategies into Action

Understanding leadership strategies and generational values is essential, but their true power lies in application. The following scenarios provide practical examples of how these strategies can be implemented in real workplace situations. Each case study highlights a specific leadership challenge, pairing it with an appropriate strategy and incorporating the generational dynamics of the staff member and leader involved.

These scenarios are designed to:

- Illustrate how leadership strategies can address barriers such as capacity, skill, or knowledge deficits.
- Show how generational values influence the approach and outcomes of leadership interventions.
- Provide actionable insights that leaders can adapt to their own teams and organizational contexts.

Through these examples, leaders can envision how to tailor their leadership approach to the unique needs of their teams, ultimately fostering a positive work environment, increasing collective efficacy, and retaining high-performing employees.

Let's dive into these case studies to see how theory becomes practice and how effective leadership transforms challenges into opportunities for growth.

Scenario: Overcoming a Will Barrier with Delegation as a Leadership Strategy

Staff Member: Michael Turner (33 years old, *Millennial*)
Leader: Ava Martinez (50 years old, *Generation X*)
Barrier: Will Barrier – Michael lacks motivation and enthusiasm to complete certain tasks, avoiding them due to disinterest and perceived lack of purpose.
Leadership Strategy: Delegation

The Situation

Michael Turner is a capable and experienced team member, but recently, his lack of enthusiasm and resistance to assigned tasks have caught the attention of Ava Martinez, his leader. Michael has been avoiding responsibilities related to organizing team meetings and preparing quarterly reports—tasks that are essential but uninspiring to him. Ava recognizes this pattern as a **will barrier**: Michael has the knowledge and capacity to complete these tasks but is choosing not to engage because of a lack of motivation and connection to the work.

As a Millennial, Michael values **purpose-driven work**, **collaboration**, and opportunities to take on meaningful challenges. He thrives when he feels his contributions align with larger organizational goals. Ava, a Generation X leader who values **pragmatism**, **efficiency**, and **results**, knows that direct intervention is necessary to address Michael's disengagement. Ava decides to implement **Delegation** as a leadership strategy to reignite Michael's sense of purpose and accountability.

The Leadership Response

Step 1: Identifying the Barrier

Ava sets up a one-on-one meeting with Michael to address his lack of engagement. Instead of framing the discussion as punitive, Ava takes a solution-oriented approach to uncover what's driving Michael's resistance.

- *Ava*: "Michael, I've noticed you've been putting off organizing the team meetings and the reports. I know you're more than capable of handling these tasks, so I want to better understand what's going on. Is there something about these responsibilities that feels unclear or unfulfilling to you?"

Michael admits that these tasks feel monotonous and disconnected from the larger goals of the team. He prefers work that challenges him, allows for creativity, and provides opportunities for growth.

Step 2: Delegating with Purpose

Understanding Michael's perspective, Ava uses **Delegation** to address the will barrier. Rather than taking the tasks away from Michael, she reassigns them with a fresh approach, connecting them to bigger-picture objectives and aligning them with Michael's desire for purpose and collaboration.

- *Ava*: "I hear you, and I want to make this work more engaging for you. Instead of simply organizing team meetings, I'd like you to lead the meetings with the goal of improving team communication and productivity. This is your opportunity to introduce creative ways to make the meetings more effective."

To further motivate Michael, Ava connects the quarterly report task to larger team outcomes:

- *Ava*: "For the quarterly reports, I'd like you to analyze the data to identify trends and make recommendations that can improve how our team performs. You're great with strategy, and I know you'll uncover insights that will help us make smarter decisions moving forward."

By reframing these tasks as opportunities for leadership and impact, Ava aligns the delegation with Michael's Millennial values of **purpose-driven work** and **growth opportunities**.

Step 3: Providing Autonomy and Accountability

Ava ensures that delegation comes with both **ownership** and **clear expectations**. She gives Michael the freedom to approach the tasks creatively while maintaining accountability for results.

- *Ava*: "I'm delegating these responsibilities to you because I trust your ability to make a real impact here. Let's set some milestones to keep us on track. I'll check in weekly to see how you're progressing, but this is your chance to take the lead."

This approach resonates with Michael's desire for autonomy and reinforces Ava's Generation X value of efficiency—holding him accountable without micromanaging.

Step 4: Following Up and Recognizing Progress

To ensure success, Ava schedules quick weekly check-ins to monitor Michael's progress, provide feedback, and address any roadblocks. This consistent follow-up helps Michael feel supported and reinforces the importance of the delegated tasks.

Ava also recognizes and praises Michael's progress publicly when he begins to deliver stronger results.

- *Ava*: "Michael's improvements to our team meetings have really made a difference in how we collaborate. His attention to detail and insights in the quarterly reports are helping us set better goals for next quarter. Great work, Michael!"

By providing public praise, Ava boosts Michael's confidence and reinforces his connection to the team's success—something Millennials value deeply.

Generational Values in Action

Ava's use of **Delegation** aligns with Michael's generational values as a Millennial:

1. **Purpose-Driven Work**: Ava reframed monotonous tasks to show how they contribute to the team's overall success and larger goals.
2. **Growth Opportunities**: Michael was given autonomy to approach the tasks creatively, allowing him to take on a leadership role and expand his skills.
3. **Collaboration and Recognition**: By publicly recognizing his work and providing opportunities to lead, Ava made Michael feel valued as a contributor to the team.

For Ava, as a Generation X leader, this strategy also aligns with her values of **results** and **efficiency**. Delegating with clear expectations ensured that progress was made without compromising the quality of the work.

The Outcome

By implementing the **Delegation** strategy, Ava transformed Michael's disengagement into enthusiasm. He embraced the opportunity to lead team meetings and analyze quarterly reports, taking pride in the meaningful impact his work had on the team.

Reflecting on the experience, Michael shared:

> "Once Ava explained how these tasks connected to our team's bigger goals, I felt a renewed sense of purpose. Being trusted to lead and contribute in my own way made all the difference."

For Ava, this outcome demonstrated the power of delegation when applied thoughtfully. By recognizing Michael's will barrier and aligning the tasks with his values, she motivated him to overcome disengagement and contribute at a higher level.

Key Takeaway

When staff members face **will barriers**, leaders can use **Delegation** to reignite motivation and accountability. By reframing tasks to connect with individual values—such as Millennials' preference for purpose-driven work, growth opportunities, and collaboration—leaders can inspire renewed engagement. Effective delegation demonstrates trust, provides ownership, and empowers staff members to contribute meaningfully to organizational success.

Scenario: Overcoming a Will Barrier with Approval/Deny as a Leadership Strategy

Staff Member: Jessica Thompson (29 years old, *Millennial*)

Leader: David Chen (45 years old, *Generation X*)

Barrier: **Will Barrier** – Jessica is struggling with aligning her actions and decisions with the organization's mission and vision. She has recently become disgruntled at work and with other staff members, often showing frustration and disengagement. She also continues to request to work on initiatives unrelated to her role while avoiding critical priorities.

Leadership Strategy: **Approval/Deny** (*Supervisory Role of Leadership*)

The Situation

Jessica Thompson is a capable and creative staff member, but her recent behavior at work has raised concerns. She has grown visibly frustrated with her role and has begun displaying signs of disengagement, such as avoiding team collaboration and expressing negativity during meetings. Jessica has also started proposing new, unrelated projects that spark her interest but do not align with the organization's vision or immediate priorities. Her disgruntled attitude is creating tension with other staff members and impacting team dynamics.

Jessica's generational values as a **Millennial**—innovation, creativity, and purpose-driven work—have made her eager to explore new and exciting opportunities. However, her focus on personal interests instead of core responsibilities has misaligned her actions with the organization's goals. David Chen, a results-driven **Generation X** leader, notices this misalignment and decides to use the **Approval/Deny** strategy under the **supervisory role of leadership** to address Jessica's behavior and realign her priorities with the organization's mission.

The supervisory role of leadership requires setting boundaries, maintaining accountability, and ensuring staff remain focused on aligned goals. By denying Jessica's unrelated project proposal and providing a clear rationale, David can redirect her focus, reset expectations, and support her in overcoming this barrier.

The Leadership Response

Step 1: Addressing Disgruntlement and Setting the Tone

David sets up a one-on-one meeting with Jessica in a private and supportive setting. He begins by acknowledging her recent frustrations and opens the floor for dialogue.

- *David*: "Jessica, I want to take a moment to talk about how things are going. I've noticed some frustration and disengagement lately, and I want to understand what's on your mind."

This approach allows Jessica to feel heard while also signaling that her behavior has not gone unnoticed. Jessica shares that she feels unchallenged in her current work and thinks her creative ideas are being overlooked.

Step 2: Clear and Direct Denial with Rationale

Once David has listened to Jessica's concerns, he addresses her recent request to pursue a side project that falls outside her current responsibilities. Using the **Approval/Deny** strategy, David clearly communicates his rationale, tying it to the lack of vision alignment and reinforcing his supervisory role as a leader.

- *David*: "I appreciate your creativity and desire to take on new challenges, but I need to deny your request to focus on this project right now. The initiative you're suggesting doesn't align with our organization's immediate vision and priorities. Right now, we need to focus on improving team collaboration and completing the critical quarterly reports, which are key to fulfilling our mission."

By providing a firm yet respectful rationale, David reinforces the importance of staying focused on tasks that align with organizational goals, which is a central responsibility of leadership in a supervisory role.

Step 3: Reinforcing Alignment with Vision and Values

David connects Jessica's core responsibilities to the bigger picture, framing her work in a way that resonates with her Millennial values of purpose and impact.

- *David*: "I know you want your work to feel meaningful and impactful, and I completely agree with that. Right now, the best way to contribute to the organization's success is by excelling in the areas where we need you most—completing the quarterly reports and collaborating with your team to improve our workflows. These tasks are essential to helping us achieve our vision of delivering efficient, high-quality results for our clients."

By reinforcing the purpose behind her core work, David helps Jessica connect her responsibilities to a larger mission, motivating her to re engage.

Step 4: Addressing Behavior and Resetting Expectations

David takes the opportunity to address Jessica's disgruntled behavior and its impact on her relationships with the team. As part of his supervisory leadership role, he communicates clear expectations while maintaining a supportive tone.

- *David*: "I also want to be honest with you—your recent frustrations have started to affect team dynamics. I want to support you and help you feel reenergized in your role, but that starts with prioritizing work that aligns with our goals and fostering a positive attitude. Let's focus on improving these areas together."

This step ensures Jessica understands the importance of both her work and her behavior in contributing to team success.

Step 5: Offering Support and Follow-Up

David makes it clear that while Jessica's proposal has been denied, he values her input and will work with her to create opportunities for professional growth. He schedules follow-ups to provide ongoing support and to hold her accountable.

- *David*: "Let's check in weekly to review your progress on the quarterly reports and to see how collaboration with the team is going. Once we've met these key priorities, we can revisit ideas for other projects and see how they align with our long-term vision. I'm here to support you every step of the way."

This shows Jessica that David is invested in her success while also reinforcing the importance of accountability under his supervisory leadership role.

Generational Values in Action

David's leadership approach incorporates both his and Jessica's generational values:

1. **Millennial Values (Jessica)**:
   - **Purpose-Driven Work**: David helps Jessica connect her core tasks to the organization's vision, showing how her work creates meaningful impact.
   - **Desire for Engagement**: David provides opportunities for dialogue, constructive feedback, and ongoing support to help reengage Jessica in her role.
2. **Generation X Values (David)**:
   - **Accountability**: David uses the Deny strategy to set boundaries and hold Jessica accountable for aligning with the organization's mission.

- **Practicality and Results**: He prioritizes critical tasks that produce measurable outcomes while keeping a firm focus on vision alignment.

The Outcome

Through the **Approval/Deny** strategy under his supervisory role, David successfully addresses Jessica's will barrier by refocusing her efforts on tasks that align with the organization's priorities. By providing a clear rationale, resetting expectations, and offering ongoing support, David helps Jessica realign her attitude and performance with the team's goals.

Over the next few weeks, Jessica works diligently to complete the quarterly reports and begins to re-engage with her team. The follow-up meetings provide her with the support she needs to stay on track, and her attitude improves as she starts to feel more purposeful in her role.

Reflecting on the experience, Jessica shares:

> "I initially felt frustrated, but David helped me understand how my work fits into the bigger picture. His feedback and support helped me reset my focus, and I feel more connected to the team and our goals now."

Key Takeaway

The **Approval/Deny** strategy, as part of the **supervisory role of leadership**, is a powerful tool for addressing will barriers, particularly when staff members exhibit behaviors or interests that lack alignment with the organization's vision. By providing a clear rationale, reinforcing alignment with mission and values, addressing behavior, and offering structured follow-up, leaders can help staff refocus, re-engage, and contribute meaningfully to organizational success.

Scenario: Overcoming a Will Barrier with Inspection as a Leadership Strategy

Staff Member: **Tyler Ramirez** (35 years old, *Millennial*)

Leader: **Monica Hayes** (50 years old, *Generation X*)

Barrier: **Will Barrier** – Tyler is showing inconsistent effort in completing his tasks and avoiding accountability for deadlines.

Leadership Strategy: **Inspection** (*Supervisory Role of Leadership*)

The Situation

Tyler Ramirez, a talented but inconsistent team member, has recently been struggling with meeting deadlines and producing work that meets the team's expectations. As a Millennial, Tyler values flexibility, autonomy, and purpose in his work. However, his relaxed approach to deadlines and occasional avoidance of responsibilities have begun to create frustration among his peers and his leader, Monica Hayes.

Monica, an experienced Generation X leader, recognizes that Tyler's inconsistent effort reflects a **will barrier**—he is choosing not to fully engage with his responsibilities. As part of her supervisory role, Monica decides to use **inspection** as a leadership strategy to address the issue. Inspection allows her to monitor Tyler's work closely and provide constructive feedback to ensure accountability. Importantly, Monica makes it clear that her intention is not to catch Tyler in a "gotcha moment" but to help him get back on track and succeed.

The Leadership Response

Step 1: Establishing the Purpose of Inspection

Monica schedules a one-on-one conversation with Tyler to discuss her concerns and introduce the inspection process in a supportive and professional manner.

- *Monica*: "Tyler, I've noticed some inconsistency with your recent deadlines and project quality. I want to work with you to identify what's going on and help you get back on track. To support you, I'll be reviewing your work more closely for a while. I want to be very clear—this isn't about catching you off guard or looking for a 'gotcha moment.' My goal is to help you succeed and provide the feedback you need to get your work back to where it should be."

Monica sets the tone by framing the inspection as a supportive, transparent process, not as a punitive measure. This approach aligns with Tyler's Millennial values, which prioritize trust, growth, and purpose-driven feedback.

Step 2: Creating a Plan for Monitoring

Monica outlines how the inspection process will work and communicates her expectations clearly. This step eliminates ambiguity and ensures Tyler understands what success looks like.

- *Monica*: "For the next few weeks, I'll be checking in on your projects at key milestones instead of waiting until the final deadline. This will allow us to review your progress together, identify any areas where you might need support, and make adjustments as needed."

Monica explains that regular check-ins are an opportunity for collaboration and improvement, not micromanagement. By breaking larger tasks into smaller, reviewable steps, Monica holds Tyler accountable while providing him with the structured support he needs.

Step 3: Conducting Inspection with Supportive Feedback

Monica begins monitoring Tyler's projects through regular check-ins. During these sessions, she asks questions about his progress, provides constructive feedback, and reinforces the importance of meeting deadlines.

- *Monica*: "Tyler, I noticed that the first draft of this report was submitted late. Let's discuss what barriers you're encountering and how we can ensure the next milestone is met on time."

Rather than scolding Tyler for missed deadlines, Monica approaches the inspection with curiosity and a problem-solving mindset. This reinforces that her intention is to help, not to criticize.

Tyler shares that he has been prioritizing tasks based on what he enjoys most, which has caused him to neglect higher-priority deadlines.

- *Monica*: "I appreciate your honesty. I understand that some tasks are less engaging, but they're still critical to the team's success. Let's create a timeline together so you can balance priorities more effectively. I'll continue to review your progress at each checkpoint to help keep you on track."

By balancing accountability with empathy, Monica motivates Tyler to improve his approach to work without feeling micromanaged.

Step 4: Reinforcing the Why

Throughout the inspection process, Monica takes the time to connect Tyler's work to the bigger picture, aligning it with his Millennial values of purpose and meaningful impact.

- *Monica*: "Tyler, your reports provide essential data that the team relies on to make key decisions. When those reports are late or incomplete, it affects everyone's ability to perform their roles effectively. Your work has a direct impact, and I want to see you succeed in contributing to the team's success."

By tying Tyler's responsibilities to the team's goals, Monica reinforces the purpose behind his tasks, which helps him reengage and take ownership of his work.

Step 5: Celebrating Improvements and Ending the Inspection

As Tyler begins to improve his consistency and meets deadlines successfully, Monica recognizes his progress and gradually reduces the level of oversight. She uses positive reinforcement to acknowledge his hard work.

- *Monica*: "Tyler, I want to acknowledge how much your consistency has improved over the past few weeks. Your work on the last project was on time and well-executed, and it made a significant difference for the team. I'm stepping back from our check-ins now because I trust that you've got this under control. Keep up the great work."

This recognition provides Tyler with a sense of accomplishment and validates his efforts. By ending the inspection process positively, Monica empowers Tyler to maintain his progress independently.

Generational Values in Action

Monica's leadership approach reflects both her and Tyler's generational values:

1. **Millennial Values (Tyler):**
   - **Purpose-Driven Work:** Monica ties Tyler's tasks to the team's success, helping him find meaning in his role.
   - **Collaborative Growth:** Monica frames the inspection as a partnership rather than punishment, which motivates Tyler to improve.
   - **Trust and Feedback:** Tyler appreciates Monica's transparency and constructive approach, which fosters trust and a sense of support.
2. **Generation X Values (Monica):**
   - **Accountability:** Monica uses inspection to ensure that expectations are being met while guiding Tyler back on track.
   - **Practical Solutions:** Monica implements a structured, milestone-based approach to monitor progress and provide timely feedback.

The Outcome

Through the **Inspection** strategy under her supervisory leadership role, Monica successfully addresses Tyler's will barrier. By clearly communicating expectations, regularly checking progress, and providing supportive feedback, Monica holds Tyler accountable while helping him improve his consistency and engagement.

Tyler not only begins meeting his deadlines but also feels more motivated and connected to his work. The inspection process helps him realize the value of prioritizing tasks and understanding their broader impact.

Reflecting on the experience, Tyler shares:

> "Monica's approach felt fair and supportive. I didn't feel like she was looking to catch me doing something wrong—she was genuinely trying to help me improve. The check-ins were a wake-up call, and they helped me get back on track."

Key Takeaway

The **Inspection** strategy, as part of the **supervisory role of leadership**, is a powerful tool for addressing will barriers by monitoring work closely, providing regular feedback, and ensuring accountability. When done transparently and with the right intent, inspection helps staff members refocus their efforts, improve performance, and reconnect with the purpose of their work. By fostering a supportive environment, leaders can guide staff toward success without creating a "gotcha" moment or a sense of distrust.

Scenario: Overcoming a Will Barrier with Communication as a Leadership Strategy

Staff Member: **Liam O'Connor** (28 years old, *Millennial*)

Leader: **Denise Collins** (45 years old, *Generation X*)

Barrier: **Will Barrier** – Liam has been disengaged in team projects and reluctant to take initiative.

Leadership Strategy: **Communication** (*Supervisory Role of Leadership*)

The Situation

Liam O'Connor, a talented but unmotivated member of the marketing team, has recently displayed a noticeable lack of enthusiasm during team meetings and projects. He has avoided volunteering for new assignments, contributing minimally to group discussions, and, at times, missing deadlines.

As a Millennial, Liam values meaningful work, collaboration, and open communication, but he has grown frustrated, feeling his ideas aren't heard or valued. This frustration has led to a **will barrier**—Liam is choosing to disengage rather than invest fully in his work.

Denise Collins, a Generation X leader and supervisor, notices the shift in Liam's behavior. Understanding the importance of proactive communication to overcome barriers, Denise decides to address the issue directly, using open and honest dialogue as her leadership strategy.

The Leadership Response

Step 1: Initiating a Private Conversation

Denise schedules a one-on-one meeting with Liam in a private and neutral setting to ensure the conversation feels supportive, not confrontational. Denise opens the discussion with care, setting a collaborative tone to encourage honesty.

- *Denise*: "Liam, I wanted to take some time to talk with you today. I've noticed that you've seemed less engaged lately during projects and team discussions. I value your input, and I want to check in with you to see how you're feeling and what's been going on."

By framing the conversation as a check-in, Denise creates a safe space for Liam to share his thoughts openly. This aligns with Millennial values of trust and transparency.

Step 2: Practicing Active Listening

Liam initially hesitates but eventually shares that he feels overlooked. He explains that in recent brainstorming sessions, his suggestions were dismissed or ignored by louder voices on the team. This has led to a sense of disconnection and resentment.

- *Liam*: "I just feel like what I say doesn't matter. I've tried offering ideas, but no one seems to take them seriously. It's hard to stay motivated when it feels like my input doesn't count."

Denise listens without interrupting, validating Liam's feelings and showing empathy. She nods and asks clarifying questions to ensure she fully understands his concerns.

- *Denise*: "I hear you, Liam, and I'm sorry you've been feeling that way. It's important to me that everyone on this team feels heard and valued. Can you tell me more about which situations stood out to you?"

By listening attentively, Denise makes Liam feel seen and respected, addressing his need for meaningful dialogue and workplace inclusion.

Step 3: Providing Honest Feedback and Encouragement

Once Liam has expressed his frustrations, Denise balances her response by acknowledging his feelings while also offering feedback to reframe his perspective.

- *Denise*: "I appreciate you being honest with me, Liam. Your input is valuable, and I don't want you to lose sight of that. I also think it's important to keep bringing your ideas to the table, even when it feels hard. Sometimes team dynamics can be challenging, but stepping back won't help you—or the team—grow."

Denise encourages Liam to remain engaged and reminds him that his voice is essential to the team's success. She offers specific examples of times when his contributions made a real impact.

- *Denise*: "Last month, the campaign design you suggested ended up being one of the most creative ideas we ran with. Your ideas add value, Liam, and I want to make sure we're creating more opportunities for you to share them."

This feedback helps Liam reconnect with his purpose and see the tangible value of his work—something Millennials deeply care about.

Step 4: Collaboratively Setting Clear Next Steps

Denise proposes solutions to ensure Liam feels more included and engaged moving forward. She also invites him to take ownership of the process by co-creating an action plan.

- *Denise*: "How about this? At our next team meeting, I'll give you the floor early in the session to share your ideas. I'll also make a point to encourage more balanced discussion so no one voice dominates the room. Would that help you feel more confident in contributing?"

Liam agrees, expressing appreciation for Denise's willingness to address the issue. Together, they discuss clear next steps:

1. **Denise will encourage open, balanced communication** during team meetings.
2. **Liam will commit to sharing his ideas** and stepping back into a more active role.
3. Denise will follow up with Liam to check on his progress and feelings in a few weeks.

Step 5: Following Up and Providing Ongoing Support

True to her word, Denise makes time to follow up with Liam after their next team meeting. She checks in to gauge how he felt about the changes and whether he noticed a difference in team dynamics.

- *Denise*: "Liam, I noticed you shared a great idea at the meeting today, and the team seemed really engaged. How did that feel for you?"

Liam responds positively, sharing that he felt heard and appreciated the opportunity to contribute. Denise continues to offer support and reinforcement moving forward, fostering a sense of trust and accountability.

Generational Values in Action

Denise's approach to communication highlights how generational values can bridge workplace barriers:

1. **Millennial Values (Liam)**:
   - **Purpose and Meaning**: Liam's need to feel that his contributions matter was addressed through validation and clear communication.
   - **Collaboration and Trust**: Denise invited Liam into the problem-solving process, reinforcing collaboration and transparency.
   - **Feedback and Encouragement**: Open dialogue and constructive feedback helped Liam reengage and feel supported.
2. **Generation X Values (Denise)**:
   - **Direct Communication**: Denise addressed the issue head-on with honesty and clarity.
   - **Pragmatic Solutions**: She offered tangible next steps to resolve the barrier and keep Liam accountable.
   - **Results-Driven Focus**: Denise balanced empathy with expectations, ensuring Liam understood his importance to the team's success.

The Outcome

By using **Communication** as a supervisory leadership strategy, Denise effectively addressed Liam's will barrier. Through open dialogue, active listening, and collaborative solutions, Denise helped Liam feel valued and reconnected to his work.

Over the following weeks, Liam's engagement improved noticeably. He began participating more actively in meetings, contributing innovative ideas, and stepping up for new assignments.

Reflecting on the experience, Liam shares:

> "Denise made me feel like my voice mattered again. Just having an honest conversation and knowing she cared made all the difference. I feel motivated to contribute, and I know my ideas have a place here."

Key Takeaway

Communication is a powerful leadership strategy within the supervisory role for addressing will barriers. By initiating open dialogue, actively listening, and providing clear feedback, leaders can uncover the root causes of disengagement and create solutions that support staff success. When leaders communicate with honesty and empathy, they foster trust, accountability, and a renewed sense of purpose in their team members.

Scenario: Overcoming a Skill Barrier with Mentorship as a Leadership Strategy

Staff Member: Maya Patel (31 years old, *Millennial*)
Leader: Brian Mitchell (50 years old, *Generation X*)
Barrier: Skill Barrier – Maya lacks confidence and proficiency in data analysis, which is critical for her role.
Leadership Strategy: Mentorship (*Coaching Role of Leadership*)

The Situation

Maya Patel, a driven and detail-oriented team member, has recently been tasked with handling data analysis reports for her department. However, Maya has little prior experience with data tools and struggles to interpret and present analytics accurately. This **skill barrier** has caused her to fall behind on deadlines and lose confidence in her abilities.

As a Millennial, Maya values opportunities for growth, hands-on learning, and collaborative support. She is eager to develop the skills necessary for success but feels overwhelmed trying to learn on her own.

Brian Mitchell, Maya's leader, is a Generation X manager who embraces a coaching mindset. Recognizing Maya's potential and the need for targeted support, Brian decides to step into a **mentorship role** to guide her through the challenge, helping her build the skills and confidence she needs to succeed.

The Leadership Response

Step 1: Identifying the Skill Barrier and Building Trust

Brian begins by scheduling a one-on-one coaching session with Maya to address her struggles openly and positively. He sets a supportive tone to ensure Maya feels safe to discuss her challenges without judgment.

- *Brian*: "Maya, I want to check in with you about the data analysis reports. I've noticed you seem a bit hesitant with them, and that's perfectly okay—it's a skill that takes time to develop. I know you're capable, so I'd like to work alongside you to help build your confidence in this area. How do you feel about that?"

By acknowledging the barrier and offering mentorship, Brian reassures Maya that struggling is part of the learning process. This aligns with Millennial values of trust, growth, and collaborative problem-solving.

Step 2: Sharing Experiences and Expertise

As an experienced leader with years of working on data analytics, Brian uses mentorship to share his knowledge in a way that Maya can apply practically. He schedules weekly coaching sessions where they work together on real reports, step by step.

- *Brian*: "When I started working with data, I found it intimidating too. Let's go through one of the reports together, and I'll show you the best way to organize and interpret the data points. I'll also share a few tips I've learned over the years that simplify the process."

During these sessions, Brian provides concrete examples, demonstrating how to:

1. Use data tools efficiently.
2. Interpret key metrics and trends.
3. Present findings in a clear, actionable way.

Brian's willingness to share his expertise and past experiences helps Maya feel less alone in her struggles and gives her practical tools to succeed.

Step 3: Providing Ongoing Feedback and Encouragement

Mentorship thrives on ongoing feedback and open communication. Throughout their sessions, Brian offers consistent, constructive feedback, helping Maya improve while celebrating her progress.

- *Brian*: "Maya, you did a great job identifying the trends in this report. Next, let's work on simplifying how you present the findings. Try summarizing the key takeaways in just two or three sentences—it'll make the report easier to digest for your audience."

Brian also provides encouragement to keep Maya motivated and engaged. By highlighting her improvements, he helps her build confidence.

- *Brian*: "I can see how much more comfortable you're becoming with these reports, Maya. Your progress has been impressive, and I'm confident you'll get to a point where this feels second nature."

Step 4: Assigning Practice Opportunities

To reinforce learning, Brian gradually increases Maya's responsibility with data analysis tasks. He assigns her manageable projects that allow her to practice her new skills with his support nearby.

- *Brian*: "For this next report, I want you to give it a try on your own. Use the strategies we've been practicing, and let's review it together before you submit. I'll be here to help if you get stuck."

This gradual release of responsibility helps Maya take ownership of her learning while knowing she has her mentor's support to fall back on.

Step 5: Reflecting on Progress and Future Development

After a few weeks of mentorship, Maya has significantly improved her data analysis skills and feels more confident tackling reports. Brian schedules a final check-in to reflect on her progress and discuss her continued growth.

- *Brian*: "Maya, I'm really proud of how far you've come. You've gained confidence and are producing solid reports now. How do you feel about your progress? Is there anything else you'd like to work on?"

Maya expresses gratitude for Brian's support and mentorship, sharing that she now feels equipped to handle data analysis independently.

- *Maya*: "I can't thank you enough, Brian. Having you guide me through the process step by step really helped me learn. I feel so much more confident now, and I actually enjoy working with the data."

Brian encourages Maya to continue practicing her skills and recommends additional resources (such as tutorials or advanced workshops) for future growth.

Generational Values in Action

Brian's mentorship approach demonstrates an understanding of generational values:

1. **Millennial Values (Maya)**:
    - **Hands-On Learning**: Maya thrives in an environment where she can learn by doing, with mentorship offering direct, practical experience.

- **Growth and Development**: Brian's guidance supports Maya's desire for skill-building and career advancement.
- **Collaboration and Trust**: Maya feels valued and supported by Brian's coaching style, which fosters trust and engagement.

2. **Generation X Values (Brian)**:
   - **Pragmatism**: Brian provides realistic, actionable steps to help Maya improve.
   - **Independent Growth**: He encourages Maya to take ownership of her learning while providing support as needed.
   - **Experience-Based Mentorship**: Brian draws on his expertise to guide Maya through challenges, sharing lessons from his own career.

The Outcome

Through mentorship as a coaching strategy, Brian helps Maya overcome her skill barrier in data analysis. By sharing his experience, providing hands-on guidance, and offering consistent feedback, Brian empowers Maya to build her proficiency and confidence.

In a follow-up reflection, Maya shares:

> "Brian's mentorship made all the difference. He didn't just tell me what to do—he showed me, supported me, and believed in me. Now, I feel confident handling data analysis on my own."

Key Takeaway

Mentorship is a powerful coaching strategy for addressing skill barriers. By sharing experiences, providing step-by-step guidance, and offering ongoing feedback, leaders can help staff develop new skills and build confidence. This strategy fosters a supportive, growth-oriented environment where employees feel empowered to succeed.

Scenario: Overcoming a Skill Barrier with Suggestions as a Leadership Strategy

Staff Member: Carlos Ramirez (30 years old, *Millennial*)
Leader: James Thompson (52 years old, *Generation X*)
Barrier: Skill Barrier – Carlos is struggling to deliver effective presentations due to underdeveloped public speaking skills.
Leadership Strategy: Suggestions (Coaching Role)

The Situation

Carlos Ramirez, a creative and dedicated team member, thrives on collaboration and opportunities for professional growth—core values of the *Millennial* generation. Recently, Carlos has been tasked with presenting project updates to clients and leadership teams. While his ideas and contributions are excellent, his presentations often fall flat due to nervous delivery, unclear messaging, and lack of confidence.

James Thompson, Carlos' leader, identifies that Carlos is experiencing a **skill barrier** related to public speaking and presentation techniques. As a *Generation X* leader, James values practical solutions, independence, and tangible results. He decides to implement **Suggestions**, a coaching strategy, to provide Carlos with actionable steps to improve his public speaking skills and gain confidence.

The Leadership Response

Step 1: Initiating a Coaching Conversation

James schedules a coaching session with Carlos to address the challenges in a supportive and solution-oriented manner. He begins the conversation by recognizing Carlos' strengths and contributions to the team.

- *James*: "Carlos, I want to say that your ideas and project work have been impressive. However, I've noticed you're struggling a bit with presentations, particularly with delivering your message clearly and confidently. Public speaking is a skill that can take time to develop, and I'd like to work with you to strengthen it."

James emphasizes that improving public speaking is a normal and achievable process, reducing any anxiety Carlos may feel. This aligns with Millennials' preference for supportive and encouraging leadership rather than critical feedback.

Step 2: Offering Clear Suggestions for Skill Improvement

James provides Carlos with specific, actionable suggestions to address his skill barrier. The suggestions are practical and tailored to Carlos' challenges with delivery, structure, and clarity.

1. **Practice with Purpose**: James encourages Carlos to rehearse his presentations multiple times out loud to build familiarity and confidence.
    - *James*: "Carlos, I suggest practicing your presentation three times before delivering it. Rehearsing out loud will help you identify areas where you can clarify your message and improve your flow."

2. **Record and Reflect**: James advises Carlos to record himself practicing a presentation to observe his tone, pace, and body language.
    - *James*: "Try recording yourself as you rehearse. Watch it back and note what works well and where you need improvement. This will give you a clearer picture of how you come across."
3. **Simplify Key Messages**: To combat Carlos' tendency to overcomplicate content, James suggests breaking presentations into three core messages or points.
    - *James*: "Focus on delivering three key takeaways for your audience. Keeping it simple will make your presentations more impactful and easier to follow."
4. **Use Visual Aids Effectively**: James recommends integrating visuals such as charts, images, or bullet points to reinforce Carlos' spoken words.
    - *James*: "Incorporate slides with visuals that align with your key points. This will help keep your audience engaged and support the message you're delivering."
5. **Seek Feedback After Practice**: James encourages Carlos to present informally to a colleague or to James himself to receive feedback in a low-pressure setting.
    - *James*: "I'd be happy to be your audience or ask another teammate to sit in. Getting feedback beforehand

can give you the confidence boost you need for the actual presentation."

Step 3: Providing Encouragement and Follow-Up

To ensure Carlos remains motivated and feels supported, James emphasizes that skill development takes time and practice. He commits to following up on Carlos' progress in a few weeks and encourages him to see challenges as opportunities to grow.

- *James*: "Don't worry if this doesn't come together perfectly overnight. Public speaking is a skill that improves with consistent practice. I'm confident you'll get there with the right focus and effort. Let's set a goal for you to implement these suggestions and touch base in two weeks to see how it's going."

James' coaching approach reflects the *Generation X* emphasis on results-driven solutions while accommodating Carlos' Millennial values—providing support, guidance, and opportunities for growth.

The Outcome

Carlos applies James' suggestions by practicing his presentation multiple times, simplifying his message, and using visual aids to clarify key points. He also records himself and seeks feedback from a trusted colleague. Over the next few weeks, Carlos begins to gain confidence in his delivery, pacing, and ability to engage his audience.

During a follow-up meeting, Carlos delivers a significantly improved presentation to James. His delivery is smoother, his message is clear, and he appears far more confident.

- *James*: "Carlos, I can see the progress you've made. Your practice and preparation really paid off. The way you structured your key points and used visuals to reinforce your ideas was excellent. Let's keep building on this success moving forward."

Carlos feels encouraged and empowered. James' thoughtful suggestions, coupled with ongoing support, gave Carlos the tools and confidence he needed to overcome his skill barrier.

- *Carlos*: "I used to feel so nervous about presenting, but breaking it down and practicing with purpose really helped. I appreciate James' support and practical advice—it made all the difference."

Key Takeaway

When staff members face **skill barriers**, the **Suggestions** strategy enables leaders to provide actionable, targeted advice that supports growth and improvement. By identifying the skill gap, offering clear, practical steps, and following up with encouragement, leaders help staff develop their abilities and build confidence.

For *Millennial* staff like Carlos, this approach aligns with their desire for guidance, growth opportunities, and meaningful support. Leaders like James, who use coaching strategies such as Suggestions, foster a culture of trust, development, and success—where staff feel empowered to learn, improve, and contribute at their highest potential.

Scenario: Overcoming a Skill Barrier with Modeling as a Leadership Strategy

Staff Member: Emily Carter (27 years old, *Millennial*)
Leader: Samantha Brooks (45 years old, *Generation X*)

Barrier: **Skill Barrier** – Emily is struggling with organizing and running effective team meetings.
Leadership Strategy: **Modeling** (Coaching Role)

The Situation

Emily Carter is a bright and enthusiastic team member who values collaboration, purpose-driven work, and professional growth—key traits of the *Millennial* generation. Emily was recently promoted to a team lead role and is responsible for running weekly team meetings. Despite her strong work ethic and excitement for the role, she struggles to organize the meetings effectively. Her meetings often lack structure, run over time, and leave the team unclear about next steps.

Samantha Brooks, Emily's leader, observes the pattern and recognizes that Emily's challenge stems from a **skill barriers in** meeting facilitation. Samantha, a *Generation X* leader, values results, efficiency, and leading by example. Rather than criticizing Emily's performance, Samantha chooses **Modeling** as a leadership strategy. By demonstrating how to run an effective meeting, Samantha aims to provide Emily with a clear, actionable example to build her skills and confidence.

The Leadership Response

Step 1: Identifying the Barrier and Offering Support

Samantha meets with Emily privately to discuss the challenges she's facing. Samantha frames the conversation positively, emphasizing that meeting facilitation is a skill that can be learned and developed.

- *Samantha*: "Emily, I want to acknowledge the effort you're putting into leading these team meetings. Stepping into a leadership role comes with a learning curve, and organizing effective meetings is a skill that takes time to master. I'd like to work with you and share some strategies to make your meetings more structured and impactful."

Emily appreciates Samantha's supportive tone and values the opportunity to grow in her role—aligning with her Millennial preference for mentorship and professional development.

Step 2: Modeling the Desired Behavior

Samantha invites Emily to observe her run the next team meeting. She explains that she will demonstrate strategies for structuring and leading an effective meeting, including time management, clarity of purpose, and actionable outcomes.

- *Samantha*: "During tomorrow's team meeting, I'll take the lead so you can observe. Pay attention to how I structure the agenda, keep the discussion focused, and ensure everyone leaves with clear next steps. Afterward, we can debrief together."

During the meeting, Samantha models the following key behaviors:

1. **Starting with a Clear Agenda**
   Samantha opens the meeting by presenting a clear, concise agenda and setting expectations for what will be covered.
   - *Samantha*: "Today, we have three priorities to discuss: project updates, deadlines for deliverables, and next steps for our new initiative. We'll spend 15 minutes on each topic to stay on track."
2. **Keeping Discussions Focused**
   Throughout the meeting, Samantha gently redirects any off-topic conversations back to the agenda, ensuring the discussion remains productive.
   - *Samantha*: "That's a great point, but let's table it for now so we can stay focused on today's priorities. We can address that in next week's meeting."

3. **Encouraging Participation**

    Samantha engages the team by asking specific questions and ensuring everyone has an opportunity to contribute.
    - *Samantha*: "I'd like to hear from each of you on this. Let's go around and share updates on where you are with your current tasks."

4. **Clarifying Next Steps**

    At the end of the meeting, Samantha summarizes key decisions, outlines clear next steps, and assigns ownership of tasks.
    - *Samantha*: "To recap, the next steps are as follows: Emily will draft the proposal by Friday, Jason will review the numbers, and I'll follow up with the client. Does everyone feel clear on what's expected?"

5. **Ending on Time**

    Samantha closes the meeting promptly, respecting everyone's time.
    - *Samantha*: "Thank you all for staying focused. We've covered everything on the agenda, so let's wrap up here."

Step 3: Debriefing and Encouraging Reflection

After the meeting, Samantha sits down with Emily to discuss what she observed. She encourages Emily to reflect on the strategies Samantha modeled and identify which ones she can implement.

- *Samantha*: "Emily, what stood out to you during the meeting? Were there any specific techniques you think you can start using in your own meetings?"
- *Emily*: "I really liked how you started with a clear agenda and kept us on track. I also noticed how you made sure everyone contributed, and ending with clear next steps helped tie everything together."

Samantha reinforces Emily's observations and provides practical advice for incorporating these techniques into her own meetings.

- *Samantha*: "That's great! Starting with a solid agenda and summarizing next steps can make a big difference. For your next meeting, I suggest you create an agenda in advance and share it with the team. Let's plan for you to facilitate next week's meeting, and I'll sit in to support you."

Step 4: Supporting Practice and Providing Feedback

The following week, Emily runs her team meeting using the strategies she learned from observing Samantha. Samantha attends as a supportive observer, offering constructive feedback afterward.

- *Samantha*: "Emily, you did a great job starting with the agenda and keeping everyone focused. I noticed you were more confident, and the team responded well to the structure. For next time, you might want to watch the clock a little more closely, but overall, this was a big step forward."

Emily feels encouraged by Samantha's feedback and continues to improve her meeting facilitation skills over time.

The Outcome

Through **Modeling**, Samantha provided Emily with a clear, real-world example of effective meeting facilitation. By observing Samantha in action, Emily gained practical strategies to structure and lead her meetings confidently.

The process empowered Emily to take ownership of her growth while feeling supported and guided by her leader. Over time, Emily's meetings became more focused, efficient, and productive, earning praise from her team and boosting her confidence as a new leader.

Key Takeaway

When staff members face **skill barriers**, **Modeling** is an effective coaching strategy that allows leaders to demonstrate the desired behaviors and provide concrete examples for success. By showing rather than telling, leaders offer clarity, build confidence, and set a standard for staff to emulate.

For *Millennial* staff like Emily, Modeling aligns with their values of mentorship, hands-on learning, and professional development. Leaders like Samantha create a supportive environment where skill barriers are addressed with empathy, guidance, and actionable strategies—empowering staff to learn, grow, and succeed.

Scenario: Overcoming a Skill Barrier with Observations as a Leadership Strategy

Staff Member: David Martinez (29 years old, *Millennial*)
Leader: Michael Reed (48 years old, *Generation X*)
Barrier: Skill Barrier – David is struggling with delivering clear and impactful client presentations.
Leadership Strategy: Observations (Coaching Role)

The Situation

David Martinez is a creative and driven team member who values collaboration, personal growth, and innovation—traits often associated with *Millennials*. As part of his role in the sales department, David frequently gives client presentations to pitch products and services. While he has strong ideas and enthusiasm, his presentations often lack structure, clarity, and confidence. Clients leave meetings with mixed understanding of the message, which has resulted in missed opportunities.

Michael Reed, David's leader, values efficiency, direct feedback, and measurable results—hallmarks of *Generation X*. Michael decides to use **Observations** as a leadership strategy to identify the specific skill gaps holding David back and provide clear, actionable feedback to improve his presentation abilities. Michael includes a **running record** to ensure his observations are objective and accurate.

The Leadership Response

Step 1: Framing the Observation

Michael schedules a one-on-one coaching session with David to discuss the skill barrier and prepare him for an upcoming client presentation. Michael explains that he will observe David's presentation during a team practice session to collect objective data.

- *Michael*: "David, I've noticed you're passionate about our products, and your creativity always stands out. However, I also sense that the structure and delivery of your presentations could be holding you back. For your next presentation, I'd like to observe you during a practice run with the team. I'll take detailed notes using a running record to give you specific feedback so we can focus on areas that need improvement. This isn't a 'gotcha moment'; it's about identifying ways I can help you sharpen this skill."

David appreciates Michael's approach, as Millennials value leaders who provide direct feedback in a constructive, supportive manner.

Step 2: Conducting the Observation

During the team's practice presentation, Michael sits in as an observer. He uses a **running record**, which involves documenting David's presentation word-for-word as well as noting key actions, such as pacing, gestures, tone, and audience engagement. This ensures Michael's feedback is objective and specific.

Michael's running record includes observations like:

- **Content**: "Introduces the product without a clear agenda. Client may not know what to expect."
- **Pacing**: "Speaks quickly, which might make it hard for clients to keep up with key points."
- **Clarity**: "Slides have too much text—overwhelms the audience. Doesn't pause to explain complex data."
- **Confidence**: "Frequent use of 'um' and 'you know' weakens delivery. Avoids eye contact during key moments."
- **Engagement**: "Few questions asked to involve the audience; feels more like a monologue."

Step 3: Providing Targeted Feedback

After the presentation, Michael schedules a follow-up coaching session to debrief. He begins by acknowledging David's strengths and effort before diving into the feedback.

- *Michael*: "David, you did a solid job showcasing your enthusiasm for the product. That passion is important, and it comes through clearly. However, I observed a few specific areas where we can fine-tune your skills to make your presentations stronger and more impactful."

Michael then uses the **running record** to share precise feedback:

1. **Clarity and Structure**
   - *Michael*: "Your presentation didn't start with an agenda, which can leave clients unclear on what to expect. Adding a brief outline at the beginning can help set the stage."
   - *Example from Running Record*: 'Introduces product without explaining the flow of the presentation.'
2. **Pacing and Delivery**
   - *Michael*: "You spoke a little too quickly, which made it hard to follow important points. Try pausing after key ideas or transitions to give your audience time to process."
   - *Observation*: 'Rapid delivery during data explanation—no pauses for emphasis.'
3. **Engagement**
   - *Michael*: "You missed opportunities to engage the audience. Asking questions like, 'Does this align with your needs?' can make the presentation feel more interactive."
   - *Observation*: 'No audience questions were posed throughout.'

4. **Confidence and Body Language**
   - *Michael*: "You used filler words like 'um' and avoided eye contact during critical moments. Practicing deliberate pauses and maintaining eye contact will make you appear more confident and in control."
   - *Observation*: 'Filler words noted 8 times; eye contact avoided when discussing pricing.'

Step 4: Co-Creating a Plan for Improvement

Michael works collaboratively with David to address these areas. Together, they develop a targeted plan:

1. **Structure the Presentation**: Start with an agenda slide and briefly explain what will be covered.
2. **Improve Pacing**: Practice slowing down and use deliberate pauses to emphasize key points.
3. **Simplify Slides**: Reduce text on slides and focus on visual elements that highlight key information.
4. **Practice Engagement**: Integrate at least three questions into the presentation to involve the audience.
5. **Strengthen Delivery**: Practice in front of a mirror or record the presentation to eliminate filler words and improve eye contact.

Michael also schedules a follow-up practice session where he will observe David's progress and offer further guidance.

Step 5: Follow-Up and Continued Support

The following week, David delivers his improved presentation during another practice session. Michael observes again, noting significant progress:

- David begins with a clear agenda.
- He paces himself more deliberately, pausing for emphasis.
- The slides are cleaner and easier to follow.
- David incorporates audience questions, creating engagement.
- His confidence shows through improved eye contact and fewer filler words.

Michael provides positive reinforcement:

- *Michael*: "David, you've made huge improvements! Starting with an agenda set the tone, and I noticed how much better your pacing and eye contact were. You also did a great job involving the audience with those questions. Let's keep refining this process, but you're definitely on the right track."

David feels motivated and supported by Michael's coaching, which aligns with his Millennial preference for clear feedback, ongoing mentorship, and collaborative problem-solving.

The Outcome

Through **Observations** and the use of a **running record**, Michael identified specific areas where David's skills needed improvement and provided targeted, actionable feedback. By focusing on clarity, pacing, engagement, and confidence, Michael helped David strengthen his presentation abilities, which ultimately led to more impactful client pitches.

David appreciated Michael's supportive approach, particularly how the feedback was clear, detailed, and constructive. Over time, David gained the skills and confidence needed to deliver polished, results-driven presentations—enhancing his performance and contributing to the team's success.

Key Takeaway

When staff face **skill barriers**, **Observations** provide leaders with objective data to pinpoint specific areas for improvement. Using tools like a **running record** ensures feedback is accurate, detailed, and actionable. Leaders can use this strategy to guide staff members toward skill mastery, helping them feel supported and capable of achieving success.

For *Millennial* staff like David, the process of observation combined with collaborative feedback aligns with their desire for mentorship, professional growth, and clarity in their development journey. By investing in the individual's success, leaders cultivate stronger, more confident team members.

Lisa Chen is a dedicated and experienced team member known for her reliability and strong work ethic—values often attributed to *Generation X*. Recently, however, Lisa has been struggling. Not only has her workload increased with multiple overlapping project deadlines, but Lisa is also facing personal challenges. She is caring for her elderly parents, coordinating doctor visits, and managing their daily care needs. Additionally, as a single parent, Lisa has the responsibility of supporting her teenage daughter, who is preparing for college entrance exams. These personal stressors have stretched Lisa's capacity thin, impacting her performance at work.

Jessica Thompson, Lisa's leader, is a Millennial who believes in fostering open communication, empathy, and positive reinforcement as core leadership values. Jessica notices Lisa's struggles—missed deadlines, uncharacteristic quietness during meetings, and a dip in work quality. Instead of pushing Lisa harder, Jessica decides to use **acknowledgement** as a leadership strategy to address the capacity barrier, supporting Lisa both professionally and personally.

The Leadership Response

Step 1: Recognizing the Barrier

Jessica first pays close attention to Lisa's behavior and performance. She notices that Lisa, who is typically punctual and engaged, has been late to a few meetings and has submitted reports with noticeable errors. Jessica also observes Lisa's withdrawn demeanor during team discussions, where she usually contributes actively.

Understanding that *Generation X* values independence and reliability, Jessica knows Lisa may not openly share her struggles. Jessica decides to have a compassionate, one-on-one conversation to recognize Lisa's contributions and open the door for support.

- *Jessica*: "Lisa, I want to check in with you because I've noticed you've been carrying a lot on your plate lately. I know how much you care about your work, and I want you to know that I see the effort you're putting in. If there's anything going on—at work or otherwise—I'm here to support you."

Lisa initially hesitates, but Jessica's empathetic approach encourages her to open up. Lisa shares her personal struggles: the challenges of balancing her parents' care, her daughter's academic pressures, and the mounting responsibilities at work. Jessica listens carefully without judgment, creating a safe space for Lisa to share her burdens.

Step 2: Public Acknowledgement During Team Meetings

Jessica decides to lift Lisa's morale by publicly acknowledging her hard work in the next team meeting. Jessica knows that *Generation X* employees like Lisa value recognition that is tied to results and effort. Public praise can remind Lisa of her value to the team while subtly reinforcing her resilience to the rest of the group.

- *Jessica (during the meeting)*: "Before we begin, I want to take a moment to acknowledge Lisa's dedication to our team and these projects. Despite some challenging timelines and personal responsibilities, Lisa has shown incredible perseverance and professionalism. Lisa, thank you for the effort you put in every day. Your contributions do not go unnoticed."

Lisa feels seen and appreciated, which boosts her morale. The praise also shifts the tone of the team meeting, fostering a supportive environment where team members recognize and appreciate one another's efforts.

Step 3: A Personal Gesture – Thank You Note

To further show her appreciation, Jessica writes Lisa a heartfelt thank-you note. She specifically highlights Lisa's strengths, contributions, and resilience while acknowledging the challenges she is facing.

Jessica's Note:

> "Lisa, I want to take a moment to thank you for everything you do—not only for our team but for your family. I know you've been juggling a lot with your parents' care and supporting your daughter during such an important time, and yet you still show up and give your best at work. Your dedication, resilience, and professionalism inspire me and the entire team. Please know that I see you, I appreciate you, and I'm here to support you however I can. You are truly an essential part of this team, and your hard work does not go unnoticed.
>
> With gratitude,
> Jessica"

Lisa receives the note and feels deeply touched. This personal acknowledgment reinforces her value as both a professional and a person. It also reminds her that her leader understands her struggles and appreciates her hard work.

Step 4: Creating Space for Dialogue and Support

After publicly and personally acknowledging Lisa, Jessica schedules a private follow-up meeting to discuss how they can adjust workloads to better accommodate Lisa's current capacity. Jessica also creates space for Lisa to share what support she needs moving forward.

- *Jessica*: "Lisa, I really value your honesty and the effort you continue to bring. Let's talk about ways we can make this workload more manageable while you're navigating personal challenges. Are there tasks we can delegate to others on the team? Would it help to extend a few of these project deadlines?"

Lisa, relieved that Jessica is offering real solutions, shares which tasks have been the most time-consuming. Jessica helps Lisa prioritize critical projects and temporarily reassigns smaller responsibilities to other team members.

- *Jessica*: "I want to make sure you have the space you need to focus on what's most important. We'll revisit these tasks weekly to ensure things are manageable for you."

Jessica's approach not only eases Lisa's workload but also reinforces that she's supported during a challenging time—both at work and in her personal life.

The Outcome

By using **acknowledgement** as a leadership strategy, Jessica effectively addressed Lisa's capacity barrier. Public praise, a personal thank-you note, and tangible workload adjustments helped Lisa feel valued, supported, and understood.

As a *Generation X* employee, Lisa deeply appreciated the recognition of her hard work and the respect for her ability to persevere despite personal challenges. With Jessica's thoughtful leadership, Lisa regained confidence and motivation. The workload adjustments allowed her to better balance her responsibilities at work and home, ultimately improving her focus and performance.

Key Takeaway

Acknowledgement is a powerful leadership strategy for addressing capacity barriers. Leaders can combine public praise, personal gestures, and genuine conversations to show appreciation and provide meaningful support. By recognizing staff members' contributions and respecting their personal challenges, leaders create a culture of empathy, trust, and motivation.

For *Generation X* staff like Lisa, this strategy aligns with their values of hard work, recognition, and personal resilience. By addressing capacity barriers with compassion and practical solutions, leaders empower staff to overcome challenges and achieve sustainable success.

Scenario: Overcoming a Capacity Barrier with Grace as a Leadership Strategy

Staff Member: **David Martinez** (45 years old, *Generation X*)
Leader: **Erin Foster** (42 years old, *Generation X*)
Barrier: **Capacity Barrier** – David is struggling to meet deadlines and maintain his usual performance due to personal challenges.
Leadership Strategy: **Grace**

The Situation

David Martinez is a dedicated and highly skilled member of the operations team. Known for his reliability, discipline, and strong sense of responsibility—hallmarks of *Generation X*—David has consistently been a top performer over the past 10 years. However, in recent weeks, David's performance has taken a noticeable dip. He's been missing deadlines, turning in incomplete work, and seems distracted during meetings.

Erin Foster, David's leader and fellow *Generation X* colleague, knows that such changes are uncharacteristic for David. Valuing accountability but also empathy, Erin decides to approach the situation with understanding and patience.

The Personal Life Challenges

When Erin schedules a private check-in, David initially hesitates to share but eventually opens up. He reveals that he's experiencing overwhelming personal challenges:

1. **His Wife's Recovery**: David's wife recently had surgery, leaving him to manage the household while also caring for her during her recovery.
2. **Caring for Children**: David has two teenage children with busy school and extracurricular schedules. Balancing

his children's needs alongside his wife's care has left him physically and emotionally exhausted.

3. **Financial Stress**: Due to additional medical bills and reduced hours his wife worked before surgery, David is also feeling financial pressure, adding to his mental burden.

David feels stretched beyond his capacity but has been reluctant to speak up out of fear of letting his team and Erin down. As a *Generation X* employee, he takes pride in his work ethic, independence, and reliability, so admitting his struggles feels deeply uncomfortable.

- *David*: "Honestly, Erin, I've been trying to keep everything together at home and work, but I just feel like I'm falling behind. My wife's recovery has been slower than we expected, and with the kids' schedules, it's been nonstop. I'm doing my best, but it feels like there aren't enough hours in the day. I hate that I'm not keeping up the way I should."

The Leadership Response

Step 1: Acknowledging David's Situation with Compassion

Erin listens carefully, showing empathy and understanding. She reassures David that sharing his struggles is not a sign of weakness but a necessary step toward finding solutions.

- *Erin*: "David, I really appreciate your honesty. I know how much you care about your work, and I can only imagine how overwhelming things must feel right now. You've been a consistent top performer for years, and it's okay to need some extra support during a challenging time."

Step 2: Offering Grace – Adjusting Expectations and Responsibilities

Understanding that David's capacity is stretched thin, Erin decides to extend **grace** by adjusting expectations, temporarily reducing his workload, and offering flexible deadlines.

- *Erin*: "Here's what we're going to do: I'm going to extend the deadlines on your two major projects by two weeks. Let's also redistribute some of your non-urgent tasks to others on the team for the time being. That will give you some space to focus on the critical work without feeling so overwhelmed."

Erin also suggests David take advantage of remote work options for the next few weeks to better balance his responsibilities at home.

- *Erin*: "If it helps, let's arrange for you to work from home a couple of days a week. That way, you can manage things at home while staying on top of your priorities here."

David visibly relaxes, appreciating Erin's willingness to help him navigate this challenging period.

Step 3: Communicating That Grace Is Not Lowering Standards

While Erin adjusts expectations, she makes it clear that this grace is not about lowering performance standards but rather supporting David through a temporary barrier. She encourages him to focus on his well-being and trust that the team will step in where needed.

- *Erin*: "David, I know it's hard for you to accept help, but you've earned this. This grace doesn't mean we're lowering expectations; it means we're being realistic and human about what you're managing right now. You're still an essential part of this team, and this is just temporary while you focus on your family."

Step 4: Following Up with Consistent Support

Erin schedules weekly check-ins to see how David is managing his adjusted workload and personal responsibilities. During these check-ins, she provides encouragement and reminds him that grace is part of a supportive leadership approach, not a reflection of his capabilities.

- *Erin*: "How are things going this week, David? Are the new deadlines helping you keep things manageable? If there's anything else you need, don't hesitate to ask."

David expresses his gratitude, sharing that the flexibility has reduced his stress and allowed him to care for his wife and children without feeling like he's falling further behind at work.

The Outcome

By extending **grace** as a leadership strategy, Erin successfully addressed David's capacity barrier. Adjusting deadlines, redistributing responsibilities, and offering remote work options gave David the breathing room he needed to focus on his family while still contributing meaningfully at work.

For David, this grace was particularly impactful because it aligned with his *Generation X* values of professionalism, accountability, and loyalty. Erin's support allowed David to maintain his dignity and pride while navigating a difficult time, and it strengthened his commitment to the team.

Within a month, David's wife recovered, and his personal responsibilities became more manageable. He returned to full capacity with a renewed sense of energy and appreciation for Erin's leadership.

- *David*: "Thank you for understanding and having my back, Erin. That flexibility made a world of difference for my family and me. I'm ready to get back on track and give 100%."

Key Takeaway

Grace is a vital leadership strategy for removing capacity barriers, particularly when staff face personal challenges. Leaders who extend grace—through adjusted expectations, flexible timelines, and empathetic support—demonstrate that they value their staff as individuals, not just employees.

For *Generation X* staff like David, this approach resonates deeply with their values of independence, loyalty, and professionalism. Grace doesn't compromise accountability; it empowers staff to overcome temporary challenges and return stronger than before.

Scenario: Overcoming a Capacity Barrier with Scheduled Check-Ins as a Leadership Strategy

Staff Member: Hannah Nguyen (27 years old, *Millennial*)
Leader: Sophia Patel (40 years old, *Millennial*)
Barrier: Capacity Barrier – Hannah is overwhelmed due to personal challenges and an increased workload.
Leadership Strategy: Scheduled Check-Ins

The Situation

Hannah Nguyen is a dedicated and skilled team member, but recently, her performance has begun to decline. Tasks are delayed, her communication has become inconsistent, and during meetings, she seems distracted and withdrawn. Sophia Patel, Hannah's leader, notices these changes and knows something is off.

Hannah, as a *Millennial*, values **work-life balance**, **collaboration**, and **continuous feedback** in the workplace. She wants to feel connected to her leader, understood as an individual, and given opportunities to succeed while managing her personal life. Sophia, also a Millennial, understands these generational values and uses them to approach Hannah's situation thoughtfully and supportively.

Sophia suspects Hannah may be experiencing a **capacity barrier**, where external personal challenges and work demands are too much to manage simultaneously. Sophia decides to implement **Scheduled Check-Ins,** a leadership strategy that allows for focused one-on-one support to help Hannah regain control and confidence.

The Leadership Response

Step 1: Initiating the Check-Ins

Sophia approaches Hannah with care and empathy, ensuring the conversation feels supportive rather than punitive. She uses a collaborative tone, reflecting Hannah's generational preference for **teamwork** and **open communication**.

- *Sophia*: "Hannah, I've noticed that things seem a little overwhelming for you right now. I want to check in and see how you're doing, and how I can help you succeed."

Sophia introduces **Scheduled Check-Ins** as a supportive measure: weekly one-on-one meetings during a time that works best for Hannah. She aligns with Hannah's Millennial value of **continuous feedback** and **flexibility** in structure.

- *Sophia*: "Let's set aside time every Tuesday afternoon for a one-on-one check-in. It'll be a space for us to talk through what's on your plate and where you might need extra support."

Step 2: Creating Structure and Support

During their first check-in, Sophia listens carefully as Hannah opens up about feeling overwhelmed. Hannah explains that personal challenges at home are impacting her energy and focus at work. With these challenges, balancing deadlines feels impossible.

Sophia respects Hannah's Millennial values of **work-life balance** and **feeling connected** by creating a supportive space for open dialogue. Sophia uses the check-in time to:

- **Prioritize tasks**: Helping Hannah identify what needs immediate attention versus what can wait.
- **Clarify expectations**: Ensuring Hannah knows where to focus her efforts to avoid overwhelm.
- **Offer reassurance**: Reminding Hannah that it's okay to ask for support and that Sophia is there to help.
- *Sophia*: "Let's break this week down into smaller steps. Focus on completing the quarterly report first, and we'll revisit the larger project during next week's check-in. This way, you're not juggling everything all at once."

Sophia ensures that Hannah feels empowered and motivated rather than micromanaged, respecting the Millennial need for **autonomy** while also providing necessary guidance.

Step 3: Consistency and Accountability

Over the following weeks, Sophia maintains the **Scheduled Check-Ins**, providing Hannah with consistency and structured time to address any challenges. These weekly conversations become a space where Hannah can openly discuss her progress, concerns, and successes.

Sophia ensures these check-ins remain supportive by:

- Offering encouragement and acknowledging Hannah's efforts.
- Following up on any agreed adjustments or priorities.
- Reassessing workloads as needed to ensure success.
- *Sophia*: "You've done a great job prioritizing your tasks this week, and I can see your progress on the report. How are you feeling about next week's workload? Let's make sure it's manageable."

This structure respects Hannah's generational need for **ongoing feedback** and **recognition,** which motivates her to stay engaged and build momentum.

Generational Values in Action

Sophia's approach aligns with key Millennial workplace values:

1. **Work-Life Balance**: By addressing Hannah's capacity concerns and helping to manage workloads, Sophia shows that she understands the importance of balance between personal and professional obligations.

2. **Continuous Feedback**: Scheduled Check-Ins offer consistent opportunities for feedback, progress updates, and reassurance, which Hannah values deeply.
3. **Collaboration and Support**: Sophia's leadership approach is not directive but collaborative. She works *with* Hannah to prioritize tasks and brainstorm solutions.
4. **Flexibility**: Offering a regular, mutually convenient time for check-ins allows Hannah the structure she needs without feeling rigid or over-managed.

The Outcome

Through consistent **Scheduled Check-Ins**, Hannah feels seen and supported. The regular communication and focused prioritization allow her to manage her capacity barrier one step at a time. With Sophia's guidance, Hannah rebuilds her confidence and begins to meet her deadlines without feeling overwhelmed.

Reflecting on the experience, Hannah shares:

> "Having those check-ins helped me feel like I wasn't alone in handling everything. Sophia gave me space to focus and set realistic goals, which helped me regain control."

For Sophia, this strategy reinforces that **Scheduled Check-Ins** are a powerful way to support staff members experiencing capacity barriers. By being intentional with time, structure, and follow-up, leaders can create an environment where staff feel valued, supported, and empowered to succeed.

Key Takeaway

When staff members face **capacity barriers**, implementing **Scheduled Check-Ins** provides a structured and supportive solution. These regular conversations allow leaders to prioritize tasks, reduce overwhelm, and provide encouragement. By honoring generational values—such as Millennials' desire for work-life balance, flexibility, and continuous feedback—leaders can foster trust and help team members achieve success.

Scenario: Overcoming a Knowledge Barrier Through Providing Professional Development

Staff Member: Olivia Bennett (28 years old, *Millennial*)
Leader: Nathan Clark (35 years old, *Millennial*)
Barrier: Knowledge Barrier – Olivia is struggling with project management skills required for her new role.
Leadership Strategy: Providing Professional Development

The Situation

Olivia Bennett is a bright and enthusiastic member of the marketing team, recently promoted to a project coordinator role. Known for her creativity, collaborative spirit, and ability to adapt quickly—traits commonly associated with *Millennials*—Olivia is eager to succeed in her new position.

However, Nathan Clark, her leader, notices that Olivia is struggling to manage deadlines, organize tasks, and communicate effectively with multiple team members on complex projects. Despite her best efforts, projects are falling behind schedule, and Olivia seems overwhelmed.

During a one-on-one coaching session, Nathan probes deeper to identify the root of the problem. Olivia admits that while she is confident in her marketing skills, she lacks formal training in project management.

- *Olivia*: "Nathan, I'm so excited about this role, but I feel like I'm learning everything on the fly. I've never had formal training in project management, and sometimes I get overwhelmed trying to keep all the moving parts in order. I want to do well, but I just don't feel confident."

Nathan recognizes that this is a **knowledge barrier** rather than a lack of effort or commitment. As a leader, Nathan decides that providing targeted **professional development** is the best way to support Olivia and equip her with the skills she needs to succeed.

The Leadership Response

Step 1: Identifying the Right Professional Development Opportunity

Nathan takes time to research training options that would directly address Olivia's knowledge gaps in project management. Understanding her *Millennial* preference for flexibility, technology, and immediate application, Nathan identifies a virtual, self-paced course on **Project Management Fundamentals** through a well-regarded online platform.

- *Nathan*: "Olivia, I've found a virtual professional development course on project management that aligns perfectly with your role. It covers task prioritization, timeline development, and team communication—exactly the areas where you need support."

Step 2: Presenting the Opportunity as an Investment

Nathan introduces the course in a positive and motivating way, framing it as an investment in Olivia's professional growth and long-term success. He emphasizes that this training will help her feel more confident, organized, and empowered in her new position.

- *Nathan*: "This isn't about pointing out what you don't know; it's about building on your strengths and giving you the tools to thrive. You've already proven that you're capable and creative—this training will help you manage the operational side of your projects with confidence."

Olivia feels encouraged and valued, knowing that Nathan is committed to her success.

Step 3: Setting Expectations and Support

Nathan sets a clear structure around the professional development, ensuring Olivia knows how to integrate the training into her workload. He adjusts her responsibilities slightly to allow time for the course and schedules regular check-ins to discuss her progress.

- *Nathan*: "Let's prioritize this course over the next month. I'll shift some tasks around so you have a couple of hours a week to focus on the training. We'll check in weekly to see how it's going and discuss any new concepts you want to implement in your projects."

Step 4: Follow-Up and Application of Learning

As Olivia progresses through the course, Nathan encourages her to share insights and apply what she learns to her current projects. During their check-ins, they discuss strategies from the training and how Olivia can use them to manage deadlines, organize tasks, and communicate more effectively with her team.

- *Nathan*: "How did the module on task prioritization go? Can you use that framework to organize the timelines for the upcoming product launch?"

Over time, Olivia begins to apply the tools and techniques from the course. She gains confidence in her ability to plan, organize, and track progress on her projects. Nathan observes a marked improvement in her performance, as deadlines are met, tasks are delegated efficiently, and her stress levels visibly decrease.

Step 2: Presenting the Opportunity as an Investment

Nathan introduces the course in a positive and motivating way, framing it as an investment in Olivia's professional growth and long-term success. He emphasizes that this training will help her feel more confident, organized, and empowered in her new position.

- *Nathan*: "This isn't about pointing out what you don't know; it's about building on your strengths and giving you the tools to thrive. You've already proven that you're capable and creative—this training will help you manage the operational side of your projects with confidence."

Olivia feels encouraged and valued, knowing that Nathan is committed to her success.

Step 3: Setting Expectations and Support

Nathan sets a clear structure around the professional development, ensuring Olivia knows how to integrate the training into her workload. He adjusts her responsibilities slightly to allow time for the course and schedules regular check-ins to discuss her progress.

- *Nathan*: "Let's prioritize this course over the next month. I'll shift some tasks around so you have a couple of hours a week to focus on the training. We'll check in weekly to see how it's going and discuss any new concepts you want to implement in your projects."

Step 4: Follow-Up and Application of Learning

As Olivia progresses through the course, Nathan encourages her to share insights and apply what she learns to her current projects. During their check-ins, they discuss strategies from the training and how Olivia can use them to manage deadlines, organize tasks, and communicate more effectively with her team.

- *Nathan*: "How did the module on task prioritization go? Can you use that framework to organize the timelines for the upcoming product launch?"

Over time, Olivia begins to apply the tools and techniques from the course. She gains confidence in her ability to plan, organize, and track progress on her projects. Nathan observes a marked improvement in her performance, as deadlines are met, tasks are delegated efficiently, and her stress levels visibly decrease.

The Outcome

By providing targeted **professional development**, Nathan successfully addressed Olivia's knowledge barrier in project management. The virtual course gave Olivia the foundational skills she needed to manage her projects effectively while aligning with her *Millennial* values of flexibility, independence, and professional growth.

Olivia now feels empowered and equipped to handle her new responsibilities, and her performance reflects this growth:

- Projects are delivered on time.
- Team communication has improved.
- Olivia exudes confidence and ownership in her role.
- *Olivia*: "Nathan, thank you for investing in me. That course gave me the tools I needed to feel in control of my projects. I'm so much more confident now, and I'm excited to keep improving."

Nathan is pleased to see Olivia thriving and knows that the decision to provide professional development not only resolved a knowledge barrier but also strengthened trust and engagement.

- *Nathan*: "You've done a fantastic job applying what you've learned, Olivia. Keep it up—this is just the beginning of where you can go."

Key Takeaway

Professional development is a powerful leadership strategy for addressing knowledge barriers. By identifying the right training opportunities and supporting staff through the learning process, leaders equip their team members with the skills and confidence needed to succeed.

For *Millennial* staff like Olivia, professional development resonates strongly with their desire for growth, flexibility, and purposeful learning. When leaders provide targeted training opportunities, they not only remove knowledge barriers but also foster engagement, motivation, and long-term success.

Scenario: Overcoming a Knowledge Barrier Through Providing Resources

Staff Member: Mason Cooper (32 years old, *Millennial*)
Leader: Karen Mitchell (48 years old, *Generation X*)
Barrier: Knowledge Barrier – Mason struggles to analyze and interpret data for team reports.
Leadership Strategy: Providing Resources

The Situation

Mason Cooper is a dedicated and hard-working member of the finance department. Known for his enthusiasm and collaborative approach—hallmarks of *Millennials*—Mason thrives when working with colleagues but struggles when tasked with analyzing and presenting financial data. Karen Mitchell, his leader, notices recurring issues in Mason's quarterly reports, where the data analysis lacks depth, and the findings are inconsistent.

In a one-on-one check-in, Karen addresses the problem directly and compassionately:

- *Karen*: "Mason, I appreciate the effort you've put into the last two reports, but I've noticed some gaps in how the data is being interpreted. I think this is a knowledge area where we can focus to help you feel more confident and accurate in your analysis. Does that resonate with you?"

Mason nods and admits that he has never received formal training in data analysis. While he understands the basics, interpreting trends, extracting insights, and using financial metrics effectively are areas where he feels unsure.

- *Mason*: "Honestly, Karen, you're right. I've never been shown the right methods to analyze this kind of data. I want to get better, but sometimes I feel like I'm just guessing."

Karen identifies this as a **knowledge barrier** and determines that providing targeted **resources** will help Mason strengthen his understanding and analytical skills without overwhelming him.

The Leadership Response

Step 1: Curating Targeted Resources

Karen takes time to find practical and accessible resources that align with Mason's knowledge gaps. Knowing that *Millennials* value on-demand learning and actionable tools, she selects:

1. A series of short **YouTube tutorials** on data interpretation and visualization techniques.
2. An **article** from a leading finance publication that explains key metrics and how to analyze them step by step.
3. A **template** for data reporting that includes examples of well-written analysis and actionable insights.

Karen ensures these resources are practical, engaging, and directly applicable to Mason's role.

Step 2: Introducing the Resources

During their next check-in, Karen presents the resources thoughtfully, framing them as tools to support Mason's growth and make his job easier:

- *Karen*: "Mason, I've found a few resources that will help you sharpen your data analysis skills. These aren't to overwhelm you but to give you practical examples of how to interpret financial trends and create clear, accurate reports."

She introduces each resource:

- *"This video series is short but thorough—it covers techniques to interpret trends, which will help you connect the numbers to a bigger story."*
- *"Here's an article that breaks down the top metrics you need to know and how to analyze them. I think this will clarify some of the confusion."*
- *"I also created a reporting template that includes examples of strong analysis. You can use it as a guide to structure your next report."*

Karen ensures Mason knows the purpose of each resource and how they address his specific challenge.

Step 3: Setting Expectations and Offering Support

Karen sets clear expectations for Mason to review the resources over the next two weeks and implement the learnings into his next report. She also reassures him that she's available to provide additional support if needed:

- *Karen*: "I'd like you to go through these resources this week and let me know what you find most helpful. Start applying some of the techniques to the data for next quarter's report. I'll be here to answer questions as you work through it, so don't hesitate to check in."

By offering resources while maintaining ongoing support, Karen ensures Mason feels empowered, not left to figure it out alone.

Step 4: Follow-Up and Feedback

After two weeks, Karen meets with Mason to discuss his progress. Mason shares that the tutorials and article helped him better understand financial metrics and spot patterns in the data. The template also provided a framework to organize his findings clearly.

Karen ensures these resources are practical, engaging, and directly applicable to Mason's role.

Step 2: Introducing the Resources

During their next check-in, Karen presents the resources thoughtfully, framing them as tools to support Mason's growth and make his job easier:

- *Karen*: "Mason, I've found a few resources that will help you sharpen your data analysis skills. These aren't to overwhelm you but to give you practical examples of how to interpret financial trends and create clear, accurate reports."

She introduces each resource:

- *"This video series is short but thorough—it covers techniques to interpret trends, which will help you connect the numbers to a bigger story."*
- *"Here's an article that breaks down the top metrics you need to know and how to analyze them. I think this will clarify some of the confusion."*
- *"I also created a reporting template that includes examples of strong analysis. You can use it as a guide to structure your next report."*

Karen ensures Mason knows the purpose of each resource and how they address his specific challenge.

Step 3: Setting Expectations and Offering Support

Karen sets clear expectations for Mason to review the resources over the next two weeks and implement the learnings into his next report. She also reassures him that she's available to provide additional support if needed:

- *Karen*: "I'd like you to go through these resources this week and let me know what you find most helpful. Start applying some of the techniques to the data for next quarter's report. I'll be here to answer questions as you work through it, so don't hesitate to check in."

By offering resources while maintaining ongoing support, Karen ensures Mason feels empowered, not left to figure it out alone.

Step 4: Follow-Up and Feedback

After two weeks, Karen meets with Mason to discuss his progress. Mason shares that the tutorials and article helped him better understand financial metrics and spot patterns in the data. The template also provided a framework to organize his findings clearly.

Mason's next report shows significant improvement:

- The analysis is clear, accurate, and ties the data to actionable insights.
- Trends are identified with confidence and communicated effectively.
- *Karen*: "Mason, your latest report is a huge step forward. The way you explained the revenue trends and linked them to the business impact was spot-on. How did you find the resources—were they helpful?"
- *Mason*: "They were a game-changer, Karen. The videos made concepts I struggled with so much clearer, and the template helped me organize my thoughts. I feel like I finally 'get it' now."

Karen praises Mason's progress and reinforces her support for his continued growth:

- *Karen*: "You did a great job applying what you learned, Mason. Let's keep building on this success. If you ever need more resources, just let me know."

The Outcome

By providing targeted **resources**—videos, articles, and a template—Karen successfully addressed Mason's knowledge barrier in data analysis. Mason now feels more confident and competent in interpreting financial trends, leading to improved performance and a stronger sense of accomplishment.

The strategy worked particularly well because it:

- Aligned with Mason's *Millennial* preference for flexible, on-demand learning.
- Gave him clear tools to apply immediately.
- Balanced autonomy with ongoing leadership support.

Mason's success not only boosts his individual confidence but also benefits the finance team by improving the quality of reporting and decision-making.

Key Takeaway

Providing resources is an effective leadership strategy for addressing knowledge barriers. By curating targeted tools like videos, articles, and templates, leaders empower staff to build their knowledge and skills in a way that is accessible and actionable.

When paired with clear expectations, follow-up, and continued support, this strategy fosters confidence, growth, and long-term success. Leaders must remember that resources should never replace actual support but instead enhance the coaching process, ensuring staff members feel valued and equipped to thrive.

CHAPTER 20

A Call to Action for Leaders of Today

Leadership is not just a role; it is a responsibility to inspire, a calling to empower, and a privilege to serve. Today's workplace demands leaders who are adaptable, empathetic, and intentional. It requires individuals willing to step beyond the boundaries of traditional management to become visionaries, mentors, and change agents. The time to act is now, and this chapter is a call to action for leaders who are ready to rise to the challenge.

1. Lead with Vision

Leadership begins with a clear and compelling vision. As a leader, your vision is the foundation upon which goals are built, strategies are implemented, and barriers are overcome. A strong vision unites individuals across generational divides and diverse backgrounds, inspiring them to contribute to something greater than themselves.

Action Step:
Take time to reflect on your organization's mission and how your leadership can drive it forward. Communicate this vision

consistently to your team, ensuring that every action aligns with the greater purpose.

2. Develop People, Not Just Processes

Leadership is ultimately about people. Your success is measured by the growth and achievements of those you lead. Invest in their development, not only by teaching skills but by nurturing their confidence, unlocking their potential, and fostering a culture of trust.

Action Step:

Implement coaching strategies from this book—mentorship, suggestions, modeling—to empower staff facing barriers. Celebrate progress and invest in professional development opportunities to encourage continuous learning.

3. Build Collective Efficacy

A high-performing team believes in its collective ability to achieve goals. This confidence doesn't happen by accident; it is cultivated through deliberate leadership strategies that encourage collaboration, mutual respect, and accountability.

Action Step:
Leverage generational insights to build bridges between team members. Promote cross-generational learning and ensure everyone feels their strengths are valued and their contributions matter.

4. Embrace Challenges as Opportunities

Every leader will encounter barriers—whether they arise from skills, will, capacity, or knowledge. True leaders see these challenges not as setbacks but as opportunities to demonstrate resilience and resourcefulness. Your response to obstacles sets the tone for your team.

Action Step:
When faced with a challenge, adopt a problem-solving mindset. Use strategies like grace, observation, or providing resources to address barriers with empathy and effectiveness.

5. Foster a Positive Workplace Culture

The most successful leaders create environments where people feel supported, respected, and motivated to do their best work. A positive culture promotes teamwork, innovation, and retention, reducing turnover and increasing satisfaction.

Action Step:
Focus on acknowledgment and communication as daily practices. Provide regular feedback, celebrate wins, and ensure transparency in your decisions. Make it clear that every team member's well-being and success matter to you.

6. Be Courageous and Accountable

Leadership requires courage—to make tough decisions, to give constructive feedback, and to hold yourself accountable for your own growth. Your willingness to lead with integrity inspires the same in your team.

Action Step:
Commit to regular self-assessment. Seek feedback from peers and staff, and make adjustments to your leadership approach as needed. Show your team that growth is a lifelong journey.

7. Legacy: Lead for the Future

The most impactful leaders create a legacy by developing the next generation of leaders. The time, energy, and care you invest in your team today will shape the organization's success for years to come.

Action Step:
Identify emerging leaders on your team. Use strategies like delegation and mentorship to prepare them for future leadership roles. Empower them with the tools and confidence to carry your vision forward.

Final Thoughts: Answering the Call

> Leadership is not easy, nor is it meant to be. It requires a commitment to learning, a dedication to others, and a willingness to adapt. This book has provided strategies to navigate barriers, build trust, and unlock potential. But knowledge alone is not enough—it is action that defines a leader.
>
> The workplace is changing, and the need for transformative leadership has never been greater. You have the tools, insights, and strategies to make a lasting impact. The time to act is now. Lead boldly, with purpose and empathy, and watch as your team achieves what once seemed impossible. This is your call to action—step into the responsibility, embrace the calling, and honor the privilege of being a leader.